B. Chirva

FOOTBALL
Goalkeepers
theoretical training

2014

УДК 796 332
Ч 64

Ч 64 **Chirva B.** Football. Goalkeepers theoretical training. –
Moscow, 2014. – 77 c.

ISBN 978-5-98724-116-5

This monograph considers main sections of
theoretical training of professional goalkeepers:
familiarization with the football regularities, analytical
preparation to the game, game plan, the analysis of played
game and gaining knowledge about various aspects of
learning and training process and health preservation.
The materials are designed for coaches working
with goalkeepers in professional football teams and youth
football.

УДК 796 332
Ч 64

ISBN 978-5-98724-185-1

CONTENTS

INTRODUCTION

Successful functioning of any professional football team suggests the acceptance of a certain, one for all procedure of sporting and usual activity by its members.

The range of main issues of functioning of professional football team, on which it is important to have the unity of players, is considerably wide. They should come to common understanding in issues on goals the team pursue, the football it's keen to play, how to train, how its living is organized in this regard and in many other things.

Difficulties here are related to the fact that players may be much different in age, experience, prowess and pace of learning ability, length of service in certain club, present different «football schools», be of different nationality. Inevitably, each of them, and firstly those possessing solid sporting experience, having played in various team under different managers, has own certain mindset on football in all of its aspects.

The theoretical training plays a critical part while developing a certain, one for all approach to various issues of the team functioning (in the context of competitive, training and social activity). It is completely subject to goalkeepers even though their play activity completely differ from that of attacking players.

Overall, the applicative knowledge is essential for goalkeepers foremost, including the specific information on playing football and training, and helping them to improve the quality of play actions explicitly and indirectly through understanding the core of training work performed. Such knowledge may include:

– football development trends and patterns, tactical tasks and players' responsibilities in different tactical schemes of play;

– principles and methods of perfection of basic components of goalkeepers' play prowess (specific anticipation reactions, technique and tactics, motor characteristics and functional capabilities);

– basics of psychological preparation;

– playing football impact on organism and injury prevention.

It has to be noted there may be goalkeepers in teams, who already ponder on coaching work in the future due to age and begin to try to understand its specificity in this regard. The theoretical training is necessary for these goalkeepers, who show interest in seeing into characteristics of training process and game construction, in significantly larger volume.

Goalkeepers' theoretical training may be exercised to a certain extent directly on course of them performing drills or training games, for example by means of certain objectives from coaches on performing some actions, error correction, prompt analysis of actions performed in one or another situation together with coaches and partners etc.

With that, it may be exercised in the pure form also: by means of special individual, group and team theoretical training, conversations, lectures, explanations, observations on matches, information reports, and also on course of goalkeepers' self-education.

The efficiency of goalkeepers theoretical training grows in case it is performed systematically according to the plan, but also taking into account established realia at the moment.

Main strands of goalkeepers theoretical training provided in the context of specially organized events (for the whole team and separately for goalkeepers) are considered in this book.

CHAPTER 1.
MAIN SECTIONS
OF GOALKEEPERS
THEORETICAL TRAINING

We may mark five main sections of work in theoretical training of professional goalkeepers:
– familiarization with the football regularities of statistical character;
– analytical preparation to the game;
– game plan;
– the analysis of played game;
– gaining knowledge about various aspects of their training and health preservation (fig. 1).

Fig. 1. Main sections of theoretical training of professional goalkeepers

Various events and variants of players' actions occur in games more or less often.

The possibility of various events and various actions performed by players while delivering the ball to the shooting position and goalscoring is determined by the football regularities identified on grounds of the analysis of statistical information of teams of high qualification play activity (in World Cups, European Championships, Russian Championships). It is due to the game regularities and biomechanical, psychomotor and physiological factors, reflecting players' technical, tactical and physical abilities.

Knowing football regularities may help goalkeepers to increase the success of play actions both directly and indirectly, by determination of proportions in work on certain components of play prowess and specific play techniques, proper organization of training as a whole.

Every competitive game is inimitable, and so the success of goalkeepers' action in game largely depends of analytical preparation to it.

Goalkeepers may perform the analytical preparation by themselves and together with coaches in the following areas: considering the specificity of a match; the analysis of information on the opponent's play construction, defining the optimal tactics of own actions in the context of the team play conception and principles, taking into account the opponents' strengths and weaknesses.

Game plans and analysis of played game are used to provide goalkeepers with a specific action plan for the oncoming game and consider how it was realized. It may be conducted at team meetings and on the individual level.

Goalkeepers should also consistently receive information on planning and tasks of trainings at certain preparation stages, connection between the training work and results of play activity, impact and meaning of certain drills, level of individual preparedness.

The special section of goalkeepers theoretical training presents the familiarization with information revealing pedagogical and medical aspects of their health preservation.

Relevance of this knowledge is due to the fact that cases of getting injured occur more often on training than in competitive games, and that even goalkeepers with a huge experienced should be protected from performing high-injury actions (random or during drills).

For notes

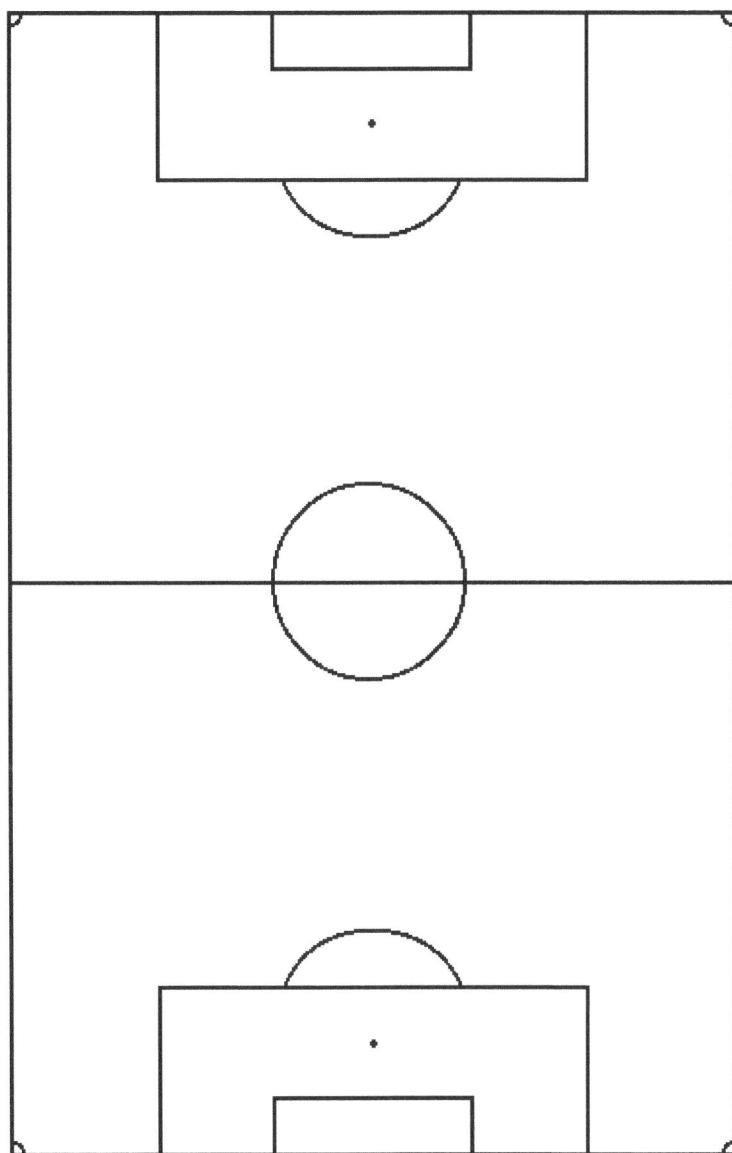

CHAPTER 2.
FAMIRIALIZATION OF
GOALKEEPERS WITH THE
FOOTBALL REGULARITIES

The football regularities reflect greater or smaller probability of various events and actions while delivering the ball to the shooting position and goalscoring, and consequently greater or smaller efficiency of one or another option of players.

Taking into account three kinds of specific goalkeeper anticipation reactions these regularities may also be classified into three groups, specifically as attributes of:

– probable course of the game and development of certain play situations;

– probable moment, speed and direction of sending the ball by players towards the goal and while shooting on goal;

– probable trajectory of the ball flying while shooting on goal.

In practice the football regularities concerning the goalscoring attacks and attacks finishing with awarding of a penalty are of the biggest interest for goalkeepers, as 75-80% of such shots at average result in goal.

2. 1. Attributes of probable course of the game and development of play situations

Knowing the major attributes of probable course of the game and development of play situations may help the success of goalkeepers in matches, including more effective conduction of defensive and attacking play. Such situations may include:

– the fact of goalscoring (conceded or scored goal);

– characteristics of goalscoring attacks and attacks resulting in awarding a penalty.

Scored and conceded goals

Statistics over the past few decades shows that number of goals in certain match at average varies from 2 to 3 in various national leagues and international competitions. This suggests high meaning of every goal for the game result.

Scored or conceded goal sufficiently impacts on goalkeepers' and players' mental health and so could turn the game to one or another side dramatically. In this regard the fact of goalscoring in football represents one of the major attributes of probable course of the game.

The most informative in this regard is the first goal in the match, exactly which team scores it and in which time period. This is explained by the following.

First. Teams that score the first goal at least don't lose in normal time in 90% of cases approximately.

Second. The impact the first goal has on the result varies depending on what minute it is scored (table 1).

There is a certain regularity consists in that first goals scored in the beginning of the first half are more important in achieving a victory.

Teams succeeding in scoring the first goal in the first 25 minutes win in one third of cases and more. In nearly the same number of cases a victory is ensured with the first goals in the game, scored from 26th minute up to the end of the match, although the duration of this time period of the game is 2.5 times longer.

It also has to be noted that first goals scored in first five minutes of the second time are significant enough in achieving a victory, while the volume of victories achieved by means of the first goal in the last minutes of the game is insignificant.

As for the second conceded goal in a row, it may already be considered as a knockout, as teams, conceding two goals in a row first, lose in more than 90% of cases, and win rarely if ever.

The possibility to change the course of the game after the first goal is due to the fact this goal has particularly strong psychic impact on the players from the both teams in first minutes after it.

Table 1. The volume of victories, draws and defeats (per cent of number of games in which goals were scored) of teams scored first in various time periods (following the normal time of 1262 games of World Cups, European Championships and Russian Championships)

Volume of victories, draws and defeats of teams scored first goals in various time periods	Time periods of the game	
	from 1st to 25th minute	from 26th to 90th minute
Volume of victories	30-45	30-43
Volume of draws	9-16	7-15
Volume of defeats	0-6	0-5

Observation reveal that in case a team concedes two goals in a row and these goals are the first and the second in the game, then the second goal is conceded within 10 minutes after the first in one third of cases (see enclosure).

It seems the second conceded goal in a row impacts on goalkeepers' and players' and their opponents' psycho-functional condition non the worse (in a negative and positive way subsequently), as the third goal is conceded within 10 «stressful» minutes after it in 40 percent of cases.

In case the team scored a goal was not able to score the second within 10 following minutes, then the team conceded a goal has the best chance to score the equalizer between ten and twenty minutes after conceding.

Statistics show the equalizer is scored approximately in quarter of cases within this time period (see enclosure).

Zones of beginning of attacks on course of the game and from set-pieces differ in probability of these attacks resulting in goal or awarding of a penalty

Goalscoring attacks and attacks resulting in awarding a penalty may begin in various zones of the pitch, though the probability of the attack finishing this way differs depending on what zone the opponent began the attacking actions in and in which way they were started: in open play or from the set-pieces.

It is pointed out by the statistics defining the efficiency of attacks (per cent of attacks resulting in goal or awarding a penalty), beginning differently in various zones of the pitch in matches of teams of high qualification (table 2).

Comparison of possibilities to score a goal and win a penalty in attacks beginning in the same zones of the pitch after tackling and interception of the ball from the opponent, from free kicks, throw-ins, shows the following (fig. 2-4).

The probability of a goal or awarding a penalty as a result of attacks beginning in the zone no further than 35 meters from the defending team goal-line in open play and from free-kicks is about the same and the highest (30 attacks are accounted for by one goal and awarding a penalty on an average).

In case attacks in this zone begin from the throw-in, the probability of a goal and awarding a penalty is several times smaller: 150 attacks are accounted for by one goal and awarding a penalty on an average.

Well-marked differences in number of attacks accounted for by one goal and awarding a penalty are evidenced when attacks begin in the attacking team defending zone or in the middle zone, in cases of the attack beginning in open play and from the set-pieces.

With attacks beginning after a tackle and interception of the ball it is approx. 1.5 times smaller than with attacks beginning with a pass from the set-pieces (100 and 150 attacks are accounted for by one goal and awarding a penalty on an average subsequently).

Table 2. The efficiency of attacks (per cent of attacks resulting in a goal or awarding a penalty) beginning in various zones of the pitch after tackling and interception the ball from the opponent, from free-kicks, throw-ins (spread of average data following games of World Cups and European Championships)

Point of the attacks beginning	Attacks beginning		
	after tackle and interception of the ball from the opponent	from free-kicks	after throw-in
Defensive zone (no further than 35 meters from the attacking team's goal-line)	1.0-1.2	0.5-0.7	0.2-0.3
Middle zone (between the attacking and defensive zones)	1.0-1.2	0.6-0.8	0.3-0.4
Attacking zone (no further than 35 meters from the defending team's goal-line)	3.0-4.0	3.0-4.0	0.5-0.6

The possibility to score a goal or win a penalty in cases when a team begins its attacks after throw-in in the zone no further than 35 meters from its goal-line is minimal (400 of such attacks are accounted for by one goal and awarding a penalty).

Taking into account a team gains around 400 cases of attacks' beginning from the defensive zone with throw-in over 50-60 games, we can say that a team may score just one goal over a competitive season as a result of such attacks.

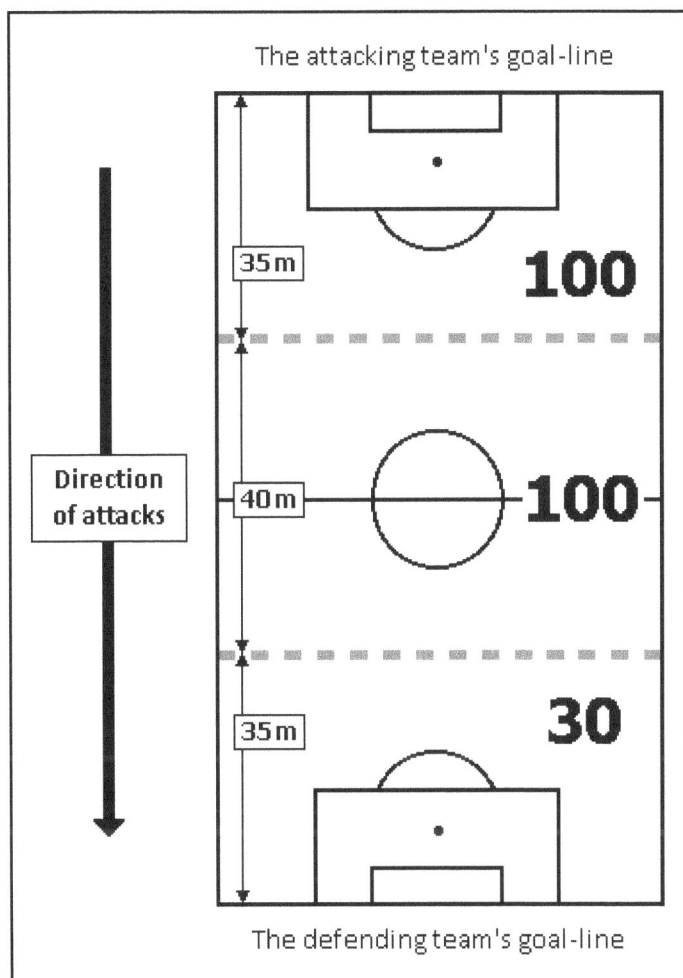

The attacking team's goal-line

35 m

100

Direction of attacks

40 m

100

35 m

30

The defending team's goal-line

Note. Numbers are rounded up to whole tens.

Fig. 2. Number of attacks beginning in different zones of the pitch after tackle and interception of the ball that is accounted for by one goal and awarding a penalty (average data following games of World Cups and European Championships)

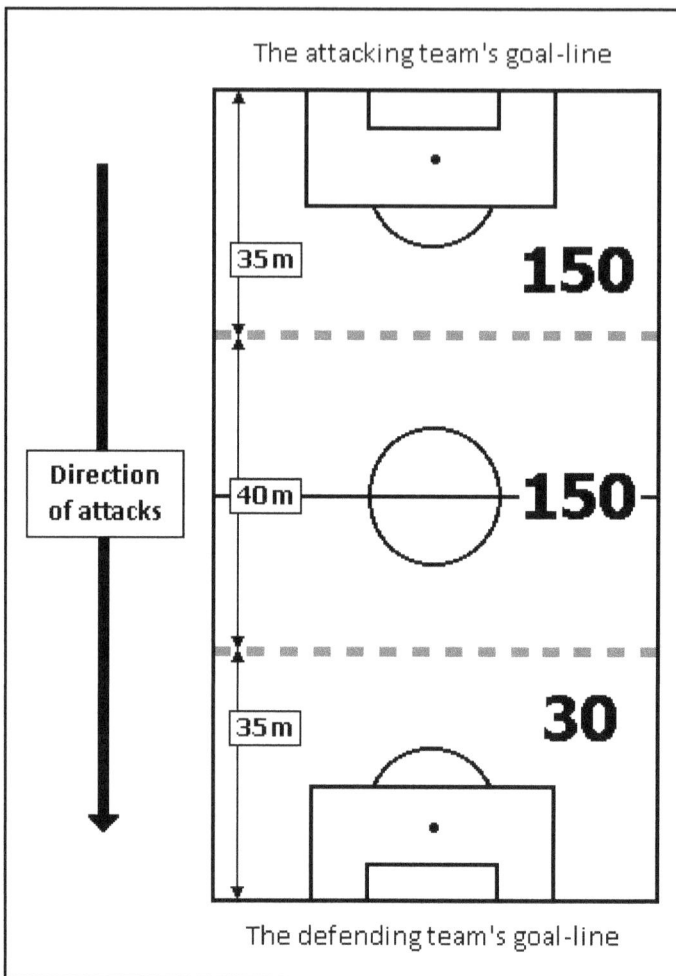

The attacking team's goal-line

Direction of attacks

35 m — 150

40 m — 150

35 m — 30

The defending team's goal-line

Note. Numbers are rounded up to whole tens.

Fig. 3. Number of attacks beginning in different zones of the pitch with set-pieces that is accounted for by one goal and awarding a penalty (average data following games of World Cups and European Championships)

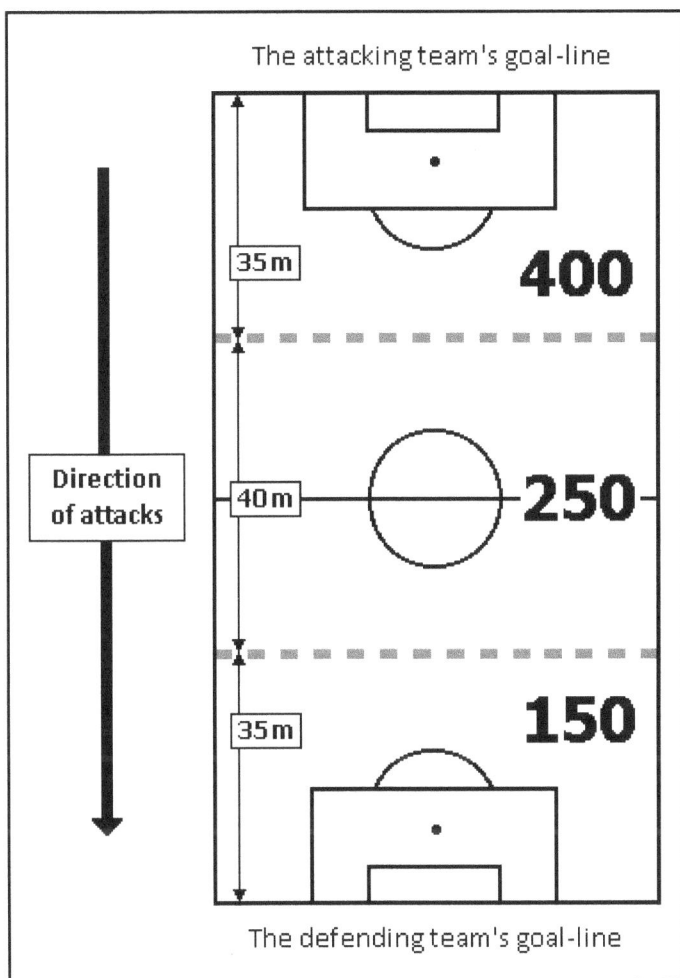

The attacking team's goal-line

35 m

400

Direction of attacks

40 m

250

35 m

150

The defending team's goal-line

Note. Numbers are rounded up to whole tens.

Fig. 4. Number of attacks beginning in different zones of the pitch after throw-in that is accounted for by one goal and awarding a penalty (average data following games of World Cups and European Championships)

Areas of beginning of goalscoring attacks on course of the game

Goalscoring attacks beginning after a tackle or interception of the ball are in the majority of all resultative attacks in football, and seemingly are the most complicated for anticipation of development by the point of beginning, as the first «move» in such attacks is not performed after the game is stopped or the ball leaves the pitch.

Most of goalscoring attacks (over 40 per cent) beginning in open play start up in the attacking team's defensive zone, a third – in the middle zone and a quarter – in the attacking zone.

Thanks to in-depth analysis of point of beginning of goalscoring attacks starting after a tackle or interception of the ball it is identified that «points of attacks initiation» are allocated over the pitch not chaotically, but concentrated in certain areas. Three such areas presenting «corridors» almost from one sideline to another are traced clear, their size along the length of the pitch is from 10 to 20 meters.

They are situated:

– one in the attacking team's defensive zone from 10 to 30 meters from its goal-line;

– the another in the middle zone from 35 to 45 meters from the attacking team's goal-line;

– the third in the attacking team's attacking zone from 20 to 35 meters from the defensive team's goal-line (fig. 5).

Speed and duration of goalscoring attacks and attacks finishing with awarding of a penalty

Speed of goalscoring attacks is approximately the same regardless in what area of the pitch they begin, while their duration depends on how far the point of the attack beginning is from the opponent's goal.

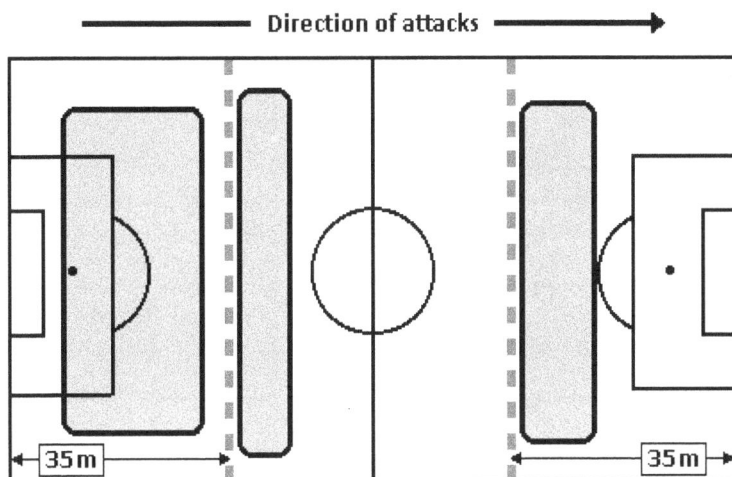

Fig. 5. Areas of the pitch from which the goalscoring attacks principally begin after a tackle or interception of the ball in matches of teams of high qualification

The duration of goalscoring attacks beginning after a tackle or interception of the ball in various areas of the pitch stands at:
– from 2 to 10 seconds in case attacks begin no further than 40 meters from the defending team's goal-line;
– from 5 to 20 seconds in case attacks begin 40 to 80 meters from the defending team's goal-line;
– from 10 to 25 seconds in case attacks begin 80 meters and more from the defending team's goal-line.
From all goalscoring attacks beginning in open play, swift-flowing attacks, which duration is no more than 15 seconds, form the most part, and also goalscoring attacks undergo during an even shorter time – no more than 10 seconds.
A little over 10 per cent fall to share of goalscoring attacks lasting more than 25 seconds (fig. 6).

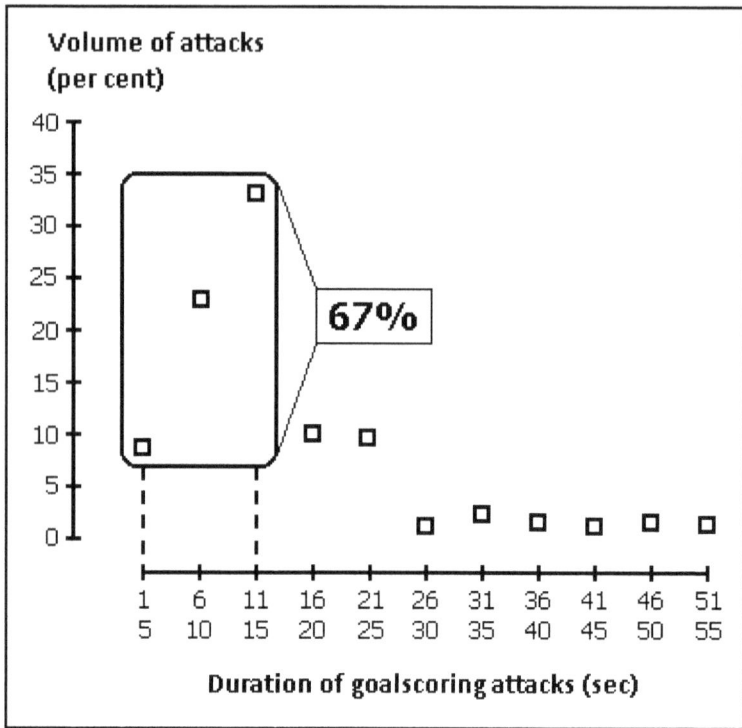

Fig. 6. The volume of goalscoring attacks of various duration, beginning after a tackle or interception of the ball (in per cent of all the goalscoring attacks beginning in open play)

From all the goalscoring attacks beginning after a break in the game or when the ball leaves the pitch, approx. 80% are attacks lasting no longer than 15 seconds (fig. 7).

Attacks finishing with a goal after a corner overwhelmingly last from 3 to 5 seconds.

The most part of attacks finishing with a goal after the ball is put into play from a set-piece is fast flowing (last no more than 15 seconds) and differ by the duration from goalscoring attacks, that begin after a tackle or interception of the ball, not by much.

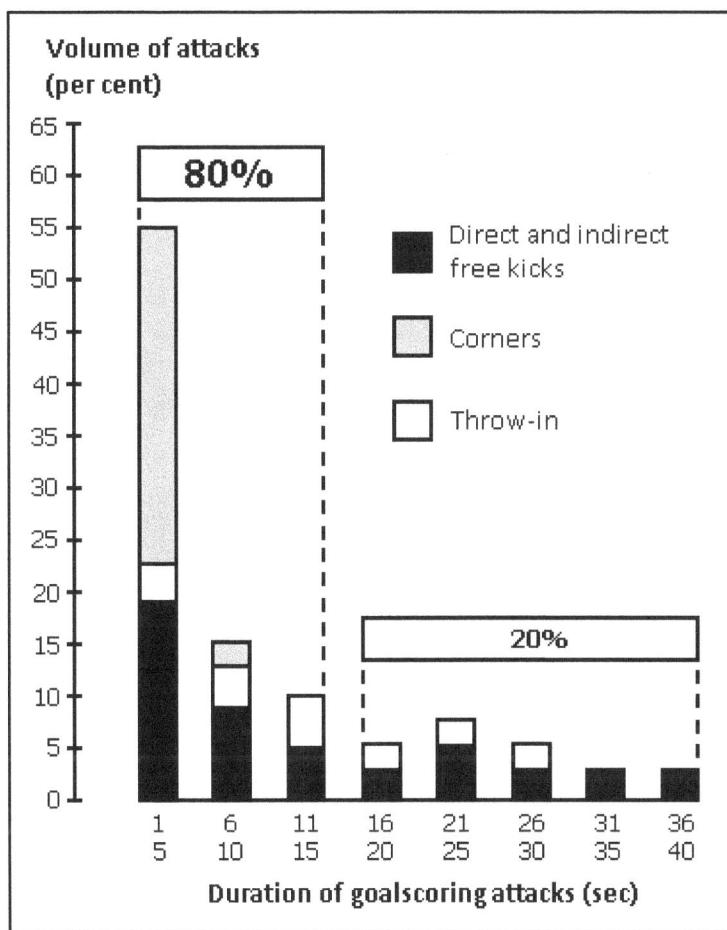

Fig. 7. The volume of goalscoring attacks of various duration beginning with a set-piece (in per cent of all the goalscoring attacks beginning with a set-piece)

Goalscoring attacks beginning with a throw-in, that generally start up in the opponent's half of the pitch, last 13 seconds at average, though the most of them last no more than 15 seconds.

Thanks to analysis of the duration of attacks finishing with awarding a penalty, it is determined that in fact they don't differ from attacks finishing with scoring a goal both by duration and point of beginning.

Number of passes performed by the team from the moment of coming over the ball until shooting on goal in goalscoring attacks

Thanks to analysis of characteristics of goalscoring attacks in games of team of high qualification it is determined that the probability of goalscoring declines along with increasing of number of passes, performed by the team from the moment of coming over the ball till shooting on goal (fig. 8).

More than a half of goals are scored in attacks when there are no more than five passes made by teams before shooting on goal. During attacks with six, seven and more passes the probability of a team scoring a goal is insignificant and approximately the same (within 2-4%).

It has to be noted that around 15% of goals in open play are scored when there were no passes at all directly before the resultative shot.

These are situations when players:

– finish attacks after interception of the ball, acting just individually (up to 5-7% of goals);

– finish off the ball bounced from the goalkeeper and players from defending and attacking teams and woodwork after a first shot on goal (up to 10-12% of goals).

Volume of goals (per cent)

```
16 ┬
14 ┤
12 ┤
10 ┤
 8 ┤
 6 ┤
 4 ┤
 2 ┤
 0 ┴  ├──┼──┼──┼──┼──┼──┼──┼──┼──┼──┤
    0  1  2  3  4  5  6  7  8  9 10 11
```

Number of passes perfomed by the team from the moment of coming over the ball till the goalscoring

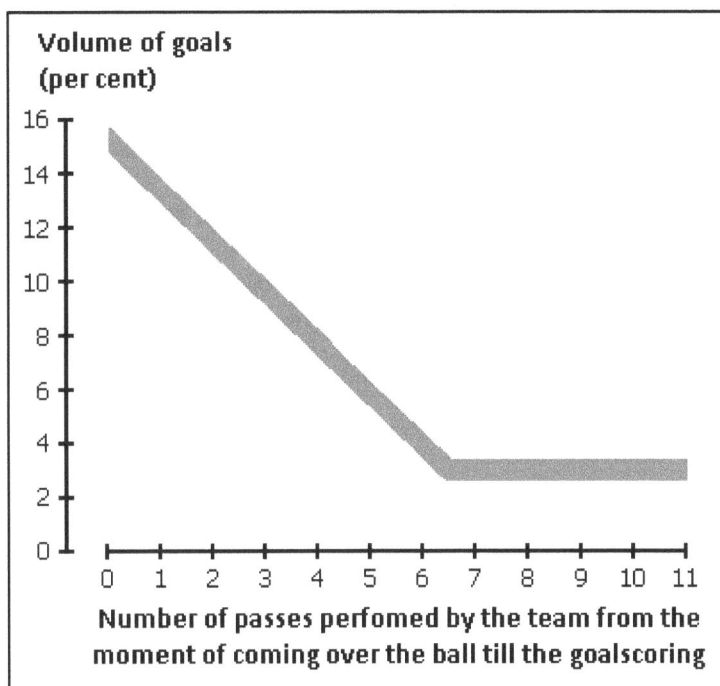

Fig. 8. Volume of goals (per cent) scored in attacks with different number of passes, performed by the team from the moment of coming over the ball till the goalscoring

Areas of performing and direction of passes, finishing with a resultative shot inside the 18-yard box

Assists are performed most often in the attacking zone (no further than 35 meters from the defending team's goal-line).

Areas from which assists are principally performed, and preferential directions of sending the ball in these cases differ depending on which conditions passes are performed in (in open play or from set-pieces), whether the ball is send for shot with a foot or head.

Since the absolute majority of goals (85% at average) in football is scored from the 18-yard box, the description of performance of those assists after which goals are scored exactly from the 18-yard box is the most essential for goalkeepers in the context of anticipation of progress of attacks that may result in goalscoring.

Performing assists from the outside of the 18-yard box into it. Assists from the outside of the 18-yard box into it in open play are generally performed from points at sidelines of the 18-yard box and from the area opposite to it almost across all its width 20-30 meters from the opponent's goal-line.

Players send the ball into the 18-yard box at angle (with or without crossing the central lengthwise axis of the pitch) or perpendicularly to the goal-line, depending on point of performing a pass across the width of the pitch, from the area opposite to the 18-yard box 20-30 meters from the opponent's goal-line (fig. 9).

Players send the ball in parallel to the goal-line or close to this direction into the area opposite to the goal 4-5 to 12-13 meters from the goal-line from areas between sidelines of the pitch and sidelines of the 18-yard box (fig. 10).

Assists into the 18-yard box from set-pieces are predominantly performed no further than 35 meters from the defending team's goal-line from the areas of irregular shape that border with sidelines of the pitch deepening into the pitch at different distance.

While performing assists from set-pieces from the attacking zone into 18-yard box the ball may be sent in parallel or at some angle to the goal-line (with or without crossing the central lengthwise axis of the pitch) with curling towards and away from the goal.

When set-pieces are performed from areas on flanks 16-30 meters from the opponent's goal-line, goals are scored more often when the ball is sent (with or without crossing the central lengthwise axis of the pitch) towards the point opposite to the middle of the goal approx. at 7 meters into the area opposite the goal from 2-3 to 10 meters from the goal-line, approx. 10 meters across the width of the pitch (fig. 11).

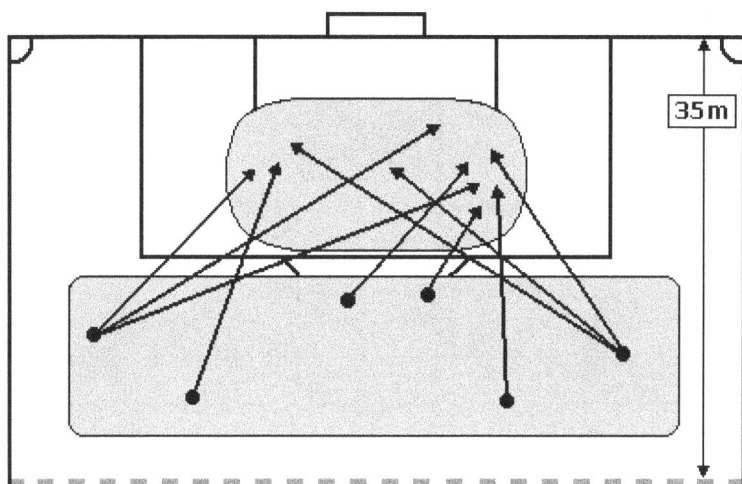

Fig. 9. Preferential directions of assists in open play into the 18-yard box from the area opposite to it 20-30 meters from the defending team's goal-line

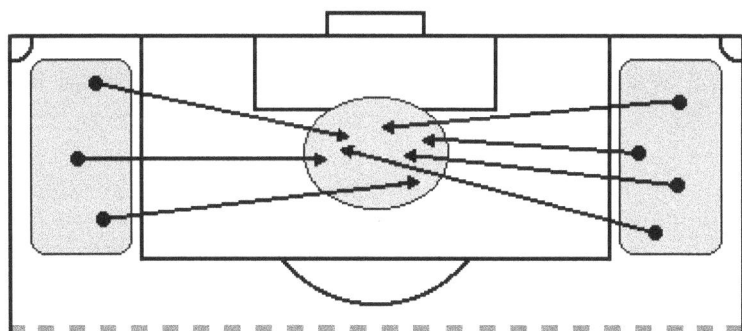

Fig. 10. Preferential directions of assists in open play into the 18-yard box from areas between sidelines of the pitch and sidelines of the defending team's 18-yard box

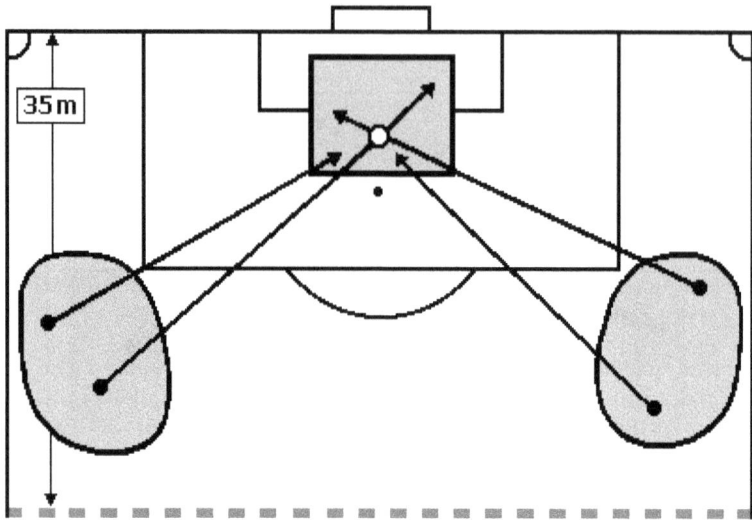

Fig. 11. Preferential directions of assists into the 18-yard box while performing set-pieces in the attacking zone from areas contiguous to sidelines of the pitch 16-30 meters from the defending team's goal-line

With assists directly from **corners** into the 18-yard box goals may be scored with a first touch from different areas of the box.

However, statistics shows that goals are scored more often with a first touch while performing corners in cases when the ball is sent into relatively small area of the 18-yard box, which lies opposite to the goal between the penalty spot and the goal area line.

This area is of the form of ellipsis positioned at some angle to the goal-line and oriented towards the corner. It begins at the goal area line opposite to the conditional point on the goal-line, which is approx. 2 meters from the near to the corner post outside the goal mouth, while its length is approx. 12 meters (fig. 12).

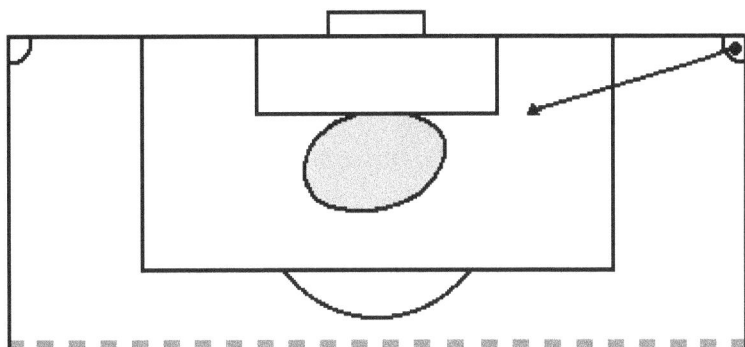

Fig. 12. The area of the 18-yard box from which goals are scored more often with a first touch after passes from the corner

Passes after which goals are scored with a **head** are overwhelmingly performed from areas between sidelines of the pitch and sidelines of the 18-yard box lengthened into the pitch.

Directions of such assists are limited with certain sectors from the left and right, because balls are sent into relatively small area (approx. 10x10 meters), positioned opposite to the goal from 2 to 10 meters from the goal-line (fig. 13).

Performing assists inside the 18-yard box. Assists in the 18-yard box are performed from two areas, each positioned to the left and to the right of the goal subsequently between the sideline of the 18-yard box and the near sideline of the goal area lengthened to the 18-yard box line.

Overwhelmingly balls are sent on a short and medium distance in parallel to the goal-line and in diagonal direction towards or away from the goal both with or without crossing the central lengthwise axis of the pitch (fig. 14).

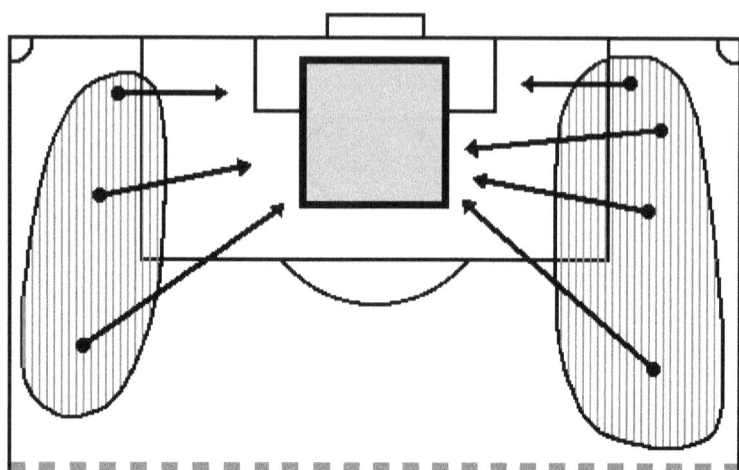

Fig. 13. Areas from which passes for goalscoring headers are performed, and preferential directions of such passes

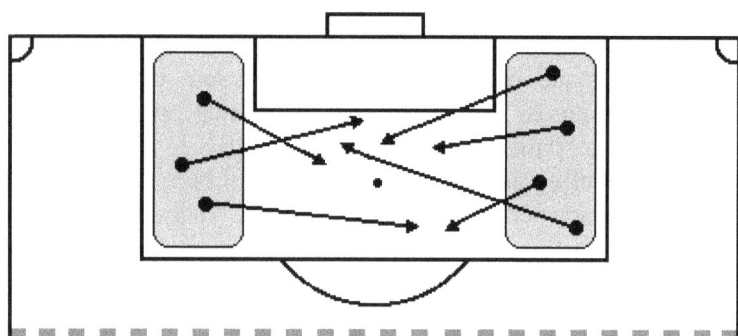

Fig. 14. Areas from which assists are performed most often in the 18-yard box, and preferential directions of such passes

Areas of performing and direction of movements with the ball finishing with a goalscoring shot in the 18-yard box

Players' movements with the ball finishing with a goalscoring shot in the 18-yard box are performed inside the box in one instance and begin from the outside of the box in another. These movements may undergo in different directions both with and without outplaying the opponent.

In case players begin movements with the ball, finishing with a goalscoring shot in the 18-yard box, from the outside of the 18-yard box, they begin their actions with the ball in the attacking zone as a rule.

Movements with the ball from the outside of the 18-yard box into it. The ball is delivered into the 18-yard box from the area opposite to it 16 to 30 meters from the defending team's goal-line for a goalscoring shot through dribbling in two directions predominantly (fig. 15):

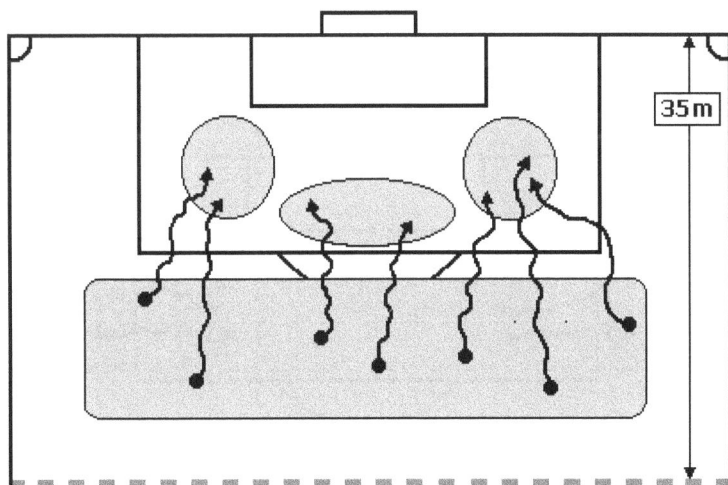

Fig. 15. Preferential directions of movements with the ball into the 18-yard box finishing with a goalscoring shot from the area

– perpendicularly or at some angle to the goal-line through corridors that may be formed by the extension of sidelines of the 18-yard box and the goal area into the areas to the left and to the right nearly between angles of the goal area and 18-yard box (in these cases shots on goal are performed with sending the ball at some angle to the direction of movement);

– perpendicularly or at some angle to the goal-line in corridor approx. 15 meters wide opposite to the goal into the area between the 18-yard box line and the penalty spot (in these cases shots on goal are performed with sending the ball into the direction coincident with the direction of dribbling or at some angle to the direction of movement).

The ball is delivered into the 18-yard box for a goalscoring shot using dribbling into areas nearly between angles of the goal area and 18-yard box from areas between sidelines of the pitch and sidelines of the 18-yard box in following directions (fig. 16):

– approx. in parallel to the goal-line;

– at some angles to the goal-line somewhat away from the goal towards the 18-yard box line.

In these cases shots on goal are performed by players with sending the ball at relatively large angles to the direction of movement with the ball before shooting.

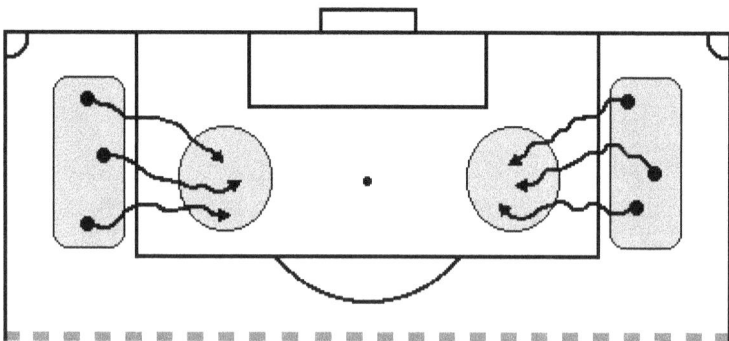

Fig. 16. Preferential directions of movements with the ball into the 18-yard box finishing with a goalscoring shot from areas between sidelines of the pitch and sidelines of the 18-yard box

Performing movements with the ball inside the 18-yard box. Movements with the ball in the 18-yard box finishing with a goalscoring shot are performed by players at relatively short distances in following directions (fig. 17):

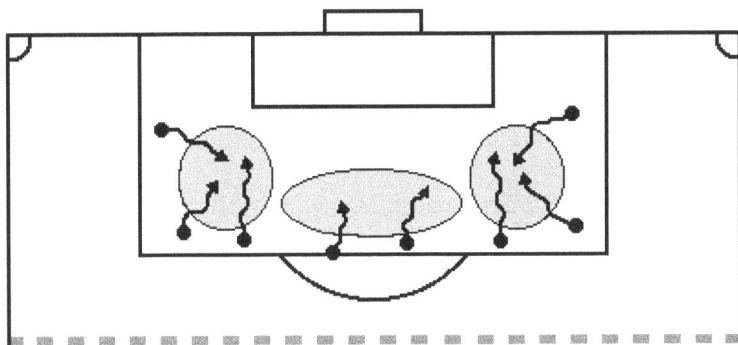

Fig. 17. Preferential directions of movements with the ball into the 18-yard box finishing with a goalscoring shot

– perpendicularly or at some angle to the goal-line between sidelines of the 18-yard box and sidelines of the goal area lengthened into the pitch into areas nearly between angles of the goal area and 18-yard box (in these cases shots on goal are performed with sending the ball at some angle to the direction of movement);

– in parallel or at some angle to the goal-line away from the goal into areas nearly between angles of the goal area and 18-yard box (in these cases shots on goal are performed with sending the ball at relatively large angle to the direction of movement);

– perpendicularly or at some angle to the goal-line in corridor approx. 15 meters wide opposite to the goal area between the 18-yard box line and the penalty spot (in these cases shots on goal are performed with sending the ball into the direction coincident with the direction of dribbling or at some angle to the direction of movement).

2. 2. Attributes of probable moment, speed and direction of sending the ball while shooting on goal

Probabilistic characteristics of moment, speed and direction of sending the ball while shooting on goal in games may include:

– critical distances for the ball hitting the target and scoring a goal;

– areas of preferential goalscoring shots performed with a foot and a head in various play situations;

– specific characteristics of performing goalscoring shots with a foot and a head in open play and from set-pieces.

Critical distance for hitting the target and goalscoring

The probability of goalscoring firstly depends on probability of the ball hitting the target.

Researches show that in sport there is a following regularity: the probability of hitting some area (target) while sending the ball decreases along with increasing of distance of shots.

There is also such regularity in football.

Percentage of the ball hitting the target (quantitative index) may change depending on the level of players' preparedness and qualification, but anyhow the decrease of precision in hitting the target happens along with the increase of shots distance. Calculations show that along with increasing the distance by 1 meters the probability of the ball hitting the target decreases by 3 per cent approximately.

Since even high class players sometimes send the ball wide from 1-2 meters, the absolute precision of the ball hitting the target in play conditions may be achieved with shooting up to 1 meter from the goal-line.

In such case the probability of the ball hitting the target with shooting from 33-35 meters is no more than 5 per cent.

This means the distance of 33-35 is critical in football in the context of probability of the ball hitting the target when players shot on goal in competitive matches (fig. 18).

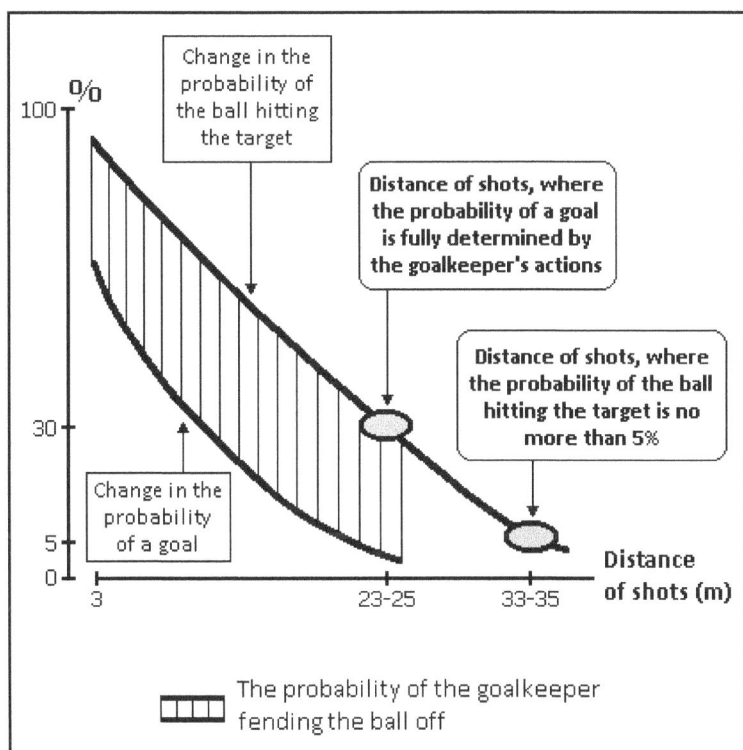

Fig. 18. Change in the probability of the ball hitting the target and of a goal (per cent) depending on the distance of shots performed by players in games

The probability of goalscoring depends not only on the probability of the ball hitting the target, but also on goalkeepers' actions.

From all the shots on target performed from the distance no further than 25 meters from the goal-line (excluding headers from the goal area and penalties) goalkeepers fend off approx. 30% regardless of the distance of a shot (table 3).

Table 3. Hitting the target, goalscoring and fending the ball off by goalkeepers (in per cent) after shooting on goal from various areas of the pitch (spread of average data following games of World Cups and European Championships)

Shots on goal	Ball hitting the target	Fending the ball off by the goalkeeper	Goal scoring
With a foot in open play from the 18-yard box	84-88	28-31	54-57
With a foot in open play from the 18-yard box (excluding the goal area)	50-54	31-34	15-20
With a foot from the outside of the 18-yard box no further than 25 meters from the goal	31-35	29-33	3-5
With a head from the 18-yard box (excluding the goal area)	33-37	30-34	4-7
Directly from free-kicks from the outside of the 18-yard box	32-37	28-33	3-6

While shooting from 23-25 meters the probability of the ball hitting the target nearly equal to the probability of goalkeepers fend off the ball (around 30%).

Therefore there is one more critical distance of shooting on goal – 23-25 meters, where the probability of a goal is in fact determined by goalkeepers' actions. We can say that goals are scored with shots performed from the distance more than 23-25 meters from the goal-line only because of goalkeepers' mistakes.

Areas from which goals are scored most often

No less than 80-85% of all goals in games of teams of high qualification are scored from the 18-yard box, with nearly 20% – directly from the goal area.

Even though more than a half of all shots on goal with foot is performed from the outside of the 18-yard box, no more than 15-20% of goals are scored with such shots, with mostly from the distance no further than 25 meters from the goal-line (fig. 19).

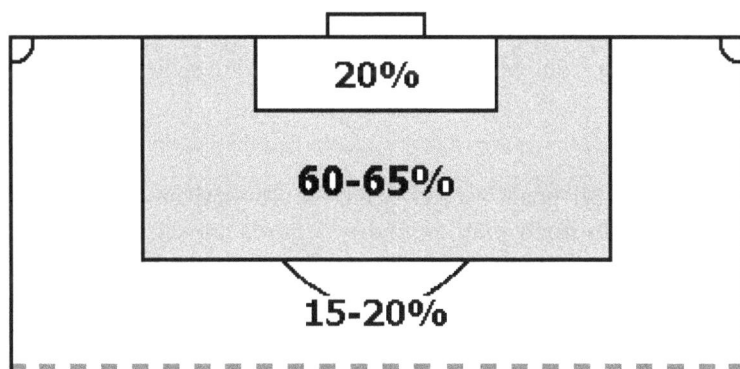

Fig. 19. Ration (in per cent) of goals scored from the goal area, 18-yard box and from the outside of the 18-yard box (following games of World Cups and European Championships)

Goals in **open play** from the outside of the 18-yard box are generally scored no further than 25 meters from the goal-line from the area opposite to the 18-yard box 30 meters wide.

Goals are scored from **set-pieces** generally from the area approx. 18-28 meters from the goal-line opposite to the goal, which is smaller in width than the 18-yard box.

Most of goals (90-95%) from the 18-yard box are scored from the oval-shaped area which is positioned from 2 meters from the goal-line to the 18-yard box line, around 25 meters across the width of the pitch and slightly displaced to the left relative to the goal from the goalkeeper's position (fig. 20).

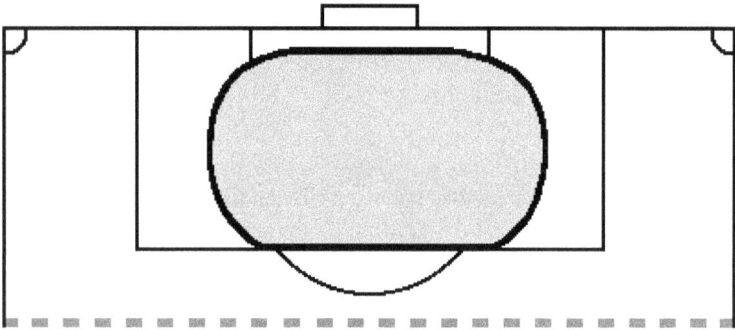

Fig. 20. Area from which the most of goals are scored in the 18-yard box

From all goals scored from the 18-yard box with shots with a **foot in open play** around two thirds are scored from the position at angle to the goal, more often from the area which is positioned to the left from the goal from the goalkeeper's position (fig. 21).

This is due to the fact that most of shots on goal with a foot in open play in the 18-yard box are performed at angle to the goal (more often from the area to the left of the goal from the goalkeeper's position), as the efficiency of such shots compared to shots from positions opposite to the goal is much lower.

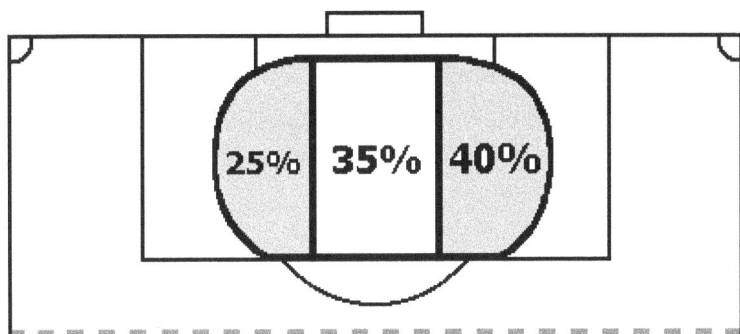

Fig. 21. Ration of goals (in per cent) scored with a foot in open play from various areas of the 18-yard box

From 80 to 90% of all **headers** are scored from the area approx. 10x10 meters, positioned opposite to the goal from 2 to 12 meters from the goal-line (fig. 22). Around a half of all headers are scored at average from the part of this area, which is situated in the goal area.

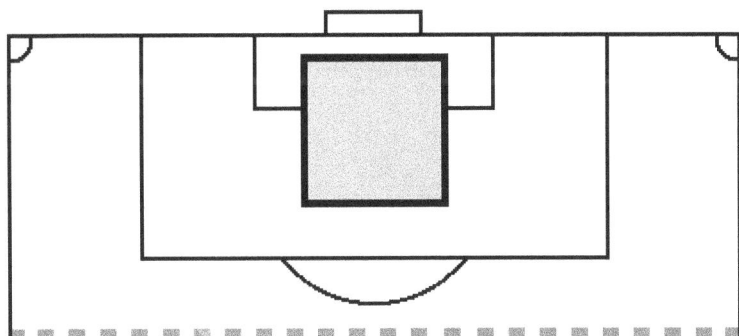

Fig. 22. Area from which the most of headers are scored

Specificity of goalscoring
shots on course of play

In the 18-yard box. Approximately each fourth or fifth goal is scored with header, 15-20% of goalscoring shots is performed while diving.

Share of goals scored as a result of finishing off the ball after its rebound off the goalkeeper, woodwork and in-field players, is 10-12% (table 4).

Table 4. Statistics defining the performance of goalscoring shots in open play within the 18-yard box

Volume of goals (%) scored with shots	
with a foot – 75-80%	with a head – 20-25%

Volume of goals (%) scored with shots	
while diving – 15-20%	without diving – 80-85%

Volume of goals (%) scored with shots	
at the rebound – 10-12%	without the rebound – 88-90%

Volume of goals (in per cent of number of goals scored with a foot) scored with a foot from the position	
at angle to the goal – 65%	opposite to the goal mouth – 35%

Volume of goals (in per cent of number of goals scored with a foot) scored with a foot a kick on the ball positioned	
on the pitch surface – 60-65%	at different heights above the pitch surface – 35-40%

If we consider goals scored with a foot only, when 35-40% of them are scored with kicks on the ball positioned at different heights above the pitch surface, and a special technique is required for performance of such kicks, as, for example, with scissor-kicks.

It has to be particularly noted that of goals scored in the 18-yard box with a foot in open play approx. two third are scored from positions at angle to the goal. Specific visually apparent characteristics are often evidenced while performing shots on goal from such positions in players' movements (position of supporting leg, actions of body, arms and kicking leg).

From the outside of the 18-yard box. Goals from the outside of the 18-yard box are scored in open play as a rule:

– after player's movements with the ball on short distance in various directions relative to the goal-line (perpendicularly, in parallel and at different angles to the goal-line);

– after passes on short and medium distances in parallel to the goal-line and away from the 18-yard box line towards the attacking team's goal.

Players may send the ball into the net with different trajectories: close to linear, mounted without curling, embowed with curling.

Specificity of goalscoring shots from free-kicks

Shots on goal from free-kicks are generally performed in conditions when players from the defending team line up the wall, closing a certain area of the goal. This stipulates that goalscoring shots from free-kicks are generally performed in two ways from the technical point of view:

a) with a most powerful shot with sending the ball without curling past the wall of defending players with an eye to the goalkeeper's mistake and to ricochet from the wall and other players (attacking and defending) positioned in the ball's way;

b) with sending the ball with an embowed trajectory with curling into the area of the goal unprotected by the goalkeeper in initial position, or into the area of the goal which is covered by the goalkeeper in initial position, though left unprotected as he begins to move in opposite point of the goal before the player shoots on goal.

Specificity of performing of a penalty

The manner of penalty kicks performance. In 10% of cases players tend to convert a penalty by means of outplaying the goalkeepers, assessing his preliminary actions and sending the ball into the unprotected area of the goal, when goalkeeper falls into unfavorable state for blocking the ball.

Overwhelmingly (90%) players execute the penalty kick with a «direct» shot ignoring goalkeeper's actions, using shots of medium power most often, less often of great and just occasionally of weak power (table 5).

Table 5. Volume of penalties (in per cent), performed in different manner and with various power

«Direct» shots			Shots with outplaying of the goalkeeper
of great power	of medium power	of weak power	
25	62	3	10

Direction of approach and sending the ball into the net While performing penalties in normal time, players send the ball into the net at some angle relative to the direction of approach towards the supporting leg nearly in 60% of cases, and exactly:

– with a right foot – to the right part of the goal from the goalkeeper;

– with a left foot – to the left part of the goal from the goalkeeper.

2. 3. Attributes of probable trajectory of the ball's flight while shooting on goal

Probabilistic characteristics of trajectories of the ball flight while shooting on goal may include:
– length of the ball trajectory in time necessary for the ball to cross the distance to the goal;
– variants of the ball trajectories.

Time of the ball's flight with a high speed at different distance

While defining the point and the moment of coming into the contact with the ball along its trajectory, goalkeepers spontaneously consider its length in time necessary for the ball to cross certain distance at a maximum speed.

It is determined that while players are kicking the static ball with a great power, it crosses distances of 25, 20 and 16,5 meters in 850, 740 and 640 msec at average.

Trajectories of the ball flight while shooting on goal

Observations reveal that several basic variants of the ball trajectory while shooting in goal occur in football practice more or less often:
– across the pitch surface and on air at different heights with a linear trajectory straight at the goalkeeper;
– across the pitch surface and on air at different heights with a linear trajectory aside from the goalkeeper;
– on air at different heights straight at the goalkeeper or aside from him with changing the initial trajectory as a result of touching the pitch surface;

– on air at different heights with a linear trajectory straight at the goalkeeper or aside from him with a sudden sharp drop in front of the goalkeeper or chaotic low-amplitude fluctuations to the left and to the right, up and down;

– across the pitch surface and on air at different heights with a linear trajectory straight at the goalkeeper or aside from him with a sudden change in initial trajectory as a result of touching by the player positioned on the ball's way;

– from some height above the pitch surface straight at the goalkeeper or aside from him with changing the initial trajectory as a result of touching the pitch surface;

– on air at different heights with an embowed trajectory of a greater or smaller ascent straight at the goalkeeper or aside from him.

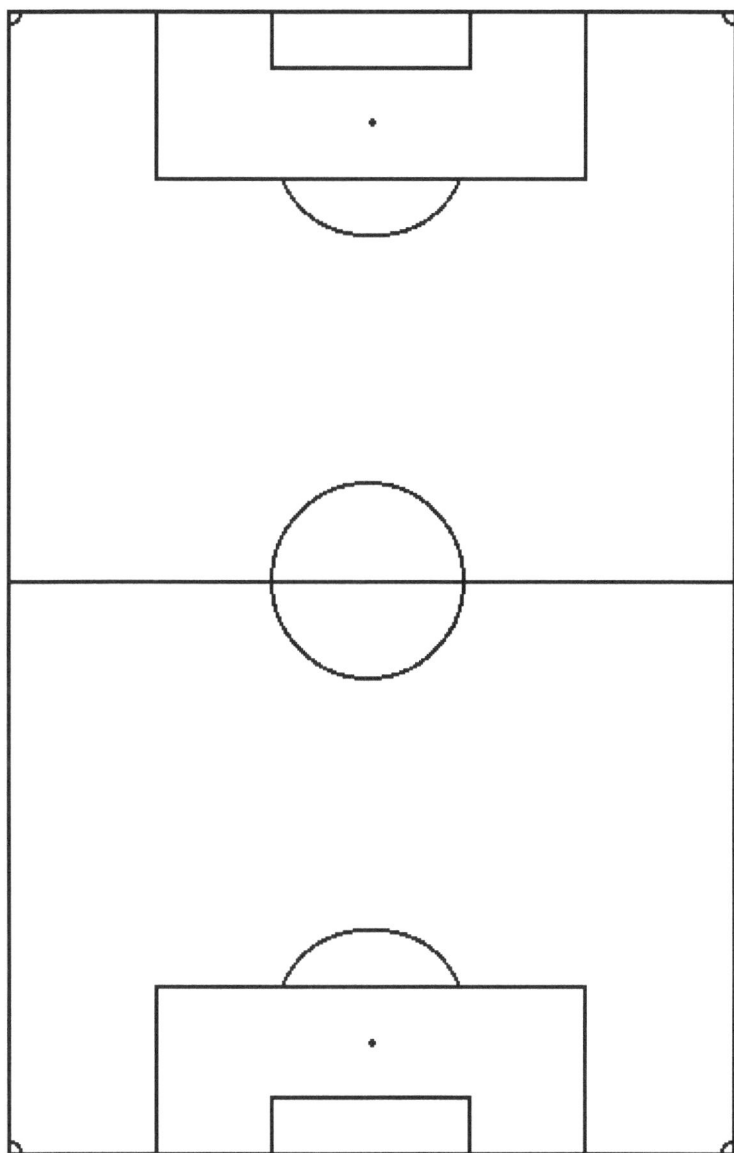

For notes

CHAPTER 3.
COACHES' ANALYTICAL
PREPARATION TO THE GAME

Each competitive game has its specificity due to the opponent's team qualification, place and time of the match, climate conditions, kind of the pitch surface, squads, importance of winning in this match, possible specific interpersonal dealings of players from opposite teams etc.

In this regard the goalkeepers preparation to the oncoming game undergo in different directions, including the analytical preparation necessarily. It is performed by them both by themselves and together with coaches in three main directions (fig. 23):

a) considering the specificity of playing the oncoming game;

b) the analysis of information on the opponent's play construction;

c) defining the optimal tactics of own actions in the game.

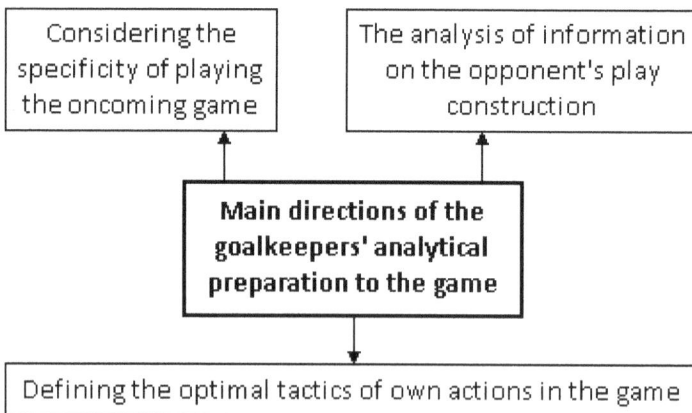

Fig. 23. Main directions of the goalkeepers' analytical preparation to the game

The practical experience of high-class goalkeepers shows that the analytical preparation to the game begins two-three days before the match as a rule.

Specificity of the game may be considered in the context of the match conditions; kind of pitch surface; possible mental pressure of the opponent fans; specific relationships between the teams, caused by many years of rivalry; presence of injured and banned attacking players in the opponent's team; manner of refereeing of the match referees.

During the analysis of the opponent's play it is reasonable for goalkeepers to give the consideration to the following main points:

– tactics of play construction in attack and defense as a whole;

– characteristics of the attacking actions in the attacking zone;

– individual merits of players involved in delivery of the ball at the shooting position and goalscoring, exactly those players able to score goals (their signature tricks, favorite positions for shooting on goal, ability to play in the air and on the rebound);

– typical variants of realization of set-pieces with participation of several players (corners, direct and indirect free kicks, throw-in in the attacking zone);

– specificity of performance of penalties and free kicks by certain players - usual performers of such kicks (with which foot and in what manner kicks are performed, with what trajectory and in which corner of the goal balls are sent).

In-depth study of the opponent's play suggests using most various possible information sources: game visuals, various internal (from club experts) and external (from the sources outside the club) statistical information on players' play activity, data from experts monitoring games, reports in media etc.

Own goalkeepers' memories on previous games with the upcoming opponent may also prove to be useful.

The consolidation of knowledge on principles of the team play construction and consideration of characteristics of the chosen team tactical game plan for the oncoming game is an important moment in analytical preparation of goalkeepers, and they informed about it at team theoretical trainings.

Therefore the thorough analysis of the opponent's play allows goalkeepers to predict optimal variants of their defensive and attacking actions in different situations in the oncoming match and simulate it at trainings together with coaches (both in special goalkeeper drills and while participating in group and team exercises).

There is usually no consistent analytical preparation for goalkeepers on a match day, though they may remember variants of their actions during the match one more time in the context of the team tactics, elaborate details of interactions with their partners, even if some tactical moments repeated in previous games more than once.

For notes

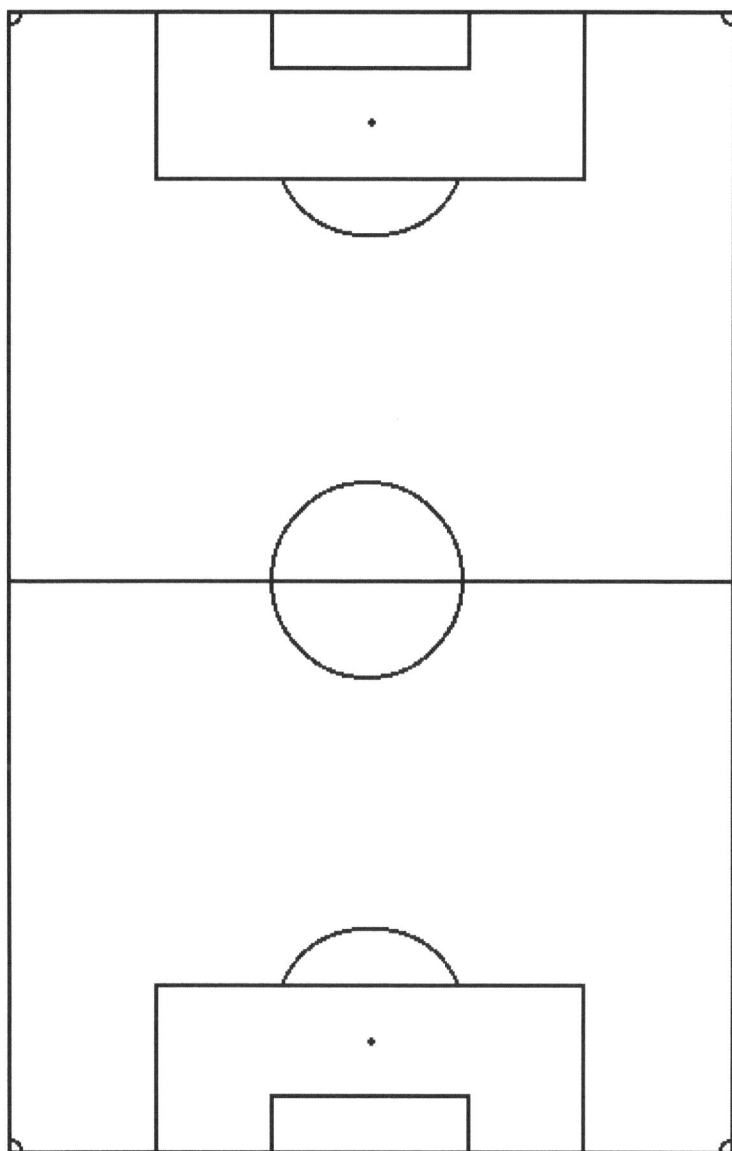

CHAPTER 4.
GAME PLAN FOR GOALKEEPERS

On a match day it is customary in football teams to perform so called game guideline a few hours before the game. The goal is to bring the team to the game all set in the theoretical and psychological context.

At the game guideline they report on the starting XI, define strengths and weaknesses of the opponent team and its certain players, present the team tactics for the match and tasks for certain players, play lines and attacking and defensive groups.

Generally the psychological and managerial task is also completed: players are motivated to display a winner mentality and to achieve victory.

The game guideline may be exercised in three ways, exactly for the whole team, certain play lines (group) and certain players (individual). These three variants of exercising the game guideline are also used for transfer of necessary information to goalkeepers.

At the whole team game guideline all players', including goalkeepers, attention is drawn to the following issues of defensive play:

– the opponent's tactics during the beginning, development and conclusion of attacks, especially in the final phase of attacking actions;

– «high», «medium» and «low» team disposal at the beginning of the opponent's attacks from the defensive zone;

– principle of the team actions in the defensive zone during the opponent's attacks on the flanks and through the middle;

– variants of opponents' actions during set-pieces (corners, free-kicks from various areas of the pitch, throw-ins in the attacking zone) and the response of own players in these situations.

Concerning the attacking actions variants of the attack beginning by goalkeepers in open play, with a goal-kick and from set-pieces in the context of the direction, distance and speed of passes in different situations may be pointed out to goalkeepers at the whole team game guideline.

Coaches may personally draw goalkeepers' attention to the necessity of performing some defensive or attacking actions to underline its meaning for realization of the chosen game plan.

At the game guideline exercised only for defenders and goalkeepers their actions in defense and attack are naturally considered in some detail with consideration of characteristics of the opponent's play. The emphasis in instructions to goalkeepers is made on their organization of defensive actions in different play situations, including the coherence of their actions with those of defenders, and also variants of the attack beginning by goalkeepers in open play, after a foul or when the ball leaves the pitch.

In individual game guideline all the possible nuances of the goalkeeper's actions in match are talked over. Particular attention is paid to the specificity of catching and blocking the ball after shots on goal and passes towards the goal taking into account the opponent's style, their individual characteristics, condition and type of the pitch surface. Also considered are the goalkeeper's behavior and possibilities of his correction of the team action in various periods of the game depending on the course of the game.

CHAPTER 5.
ANALYZING THE GAME
WITH GOALKEEPERS

Professional football is not just a football game, it is football game in the context of some competition. So each competitive game presents another step towards achieving certain final result by the team in competition (taking certain position).

In this regard both players and goalkeepers having played the match players should definitely know what «gaming step» have they took and how they can perform the following «gaming step» more confidently. They may timely get answers to these questions with quite systematic exercising of such special theoretical trainings as the game analysis.

5. 1. The significance of the game analysis for increasing the level of goalkeepers' prowess

The approach to the frequency of the game analysis suggesting the analysis of each played game is the most preferential for goalkeepers of professional teams. This is due to the fact that regular game analyzing is the effective recipe of increasing of the goalkeepers' prowess, firstly the level of their tactical qualification, due to several reasons (fig. 24).

Firstly, the game analysis with goalkeepers may be performed a relatively high number of times a season. There may be around 40-50 of them, as there are friendlies on course of pre-season, in the break between competition stages, in certain cycles between games, except competitive matches.

Secondly, thanks to relatively large amount of game analysis it is possible to consistently and intentionally improve various components of goalkeepers' preparedness and play.

| Relatively high number of game analyzes | Objectivity of the information provided |

Factors defining the significance of the game analysis with goalkeepers

| Possibility to vary volumes of incentive and critical information | Possibility of permanent and focused play perfection |

Individualization of information traslation process and its analysis by goalkeepers

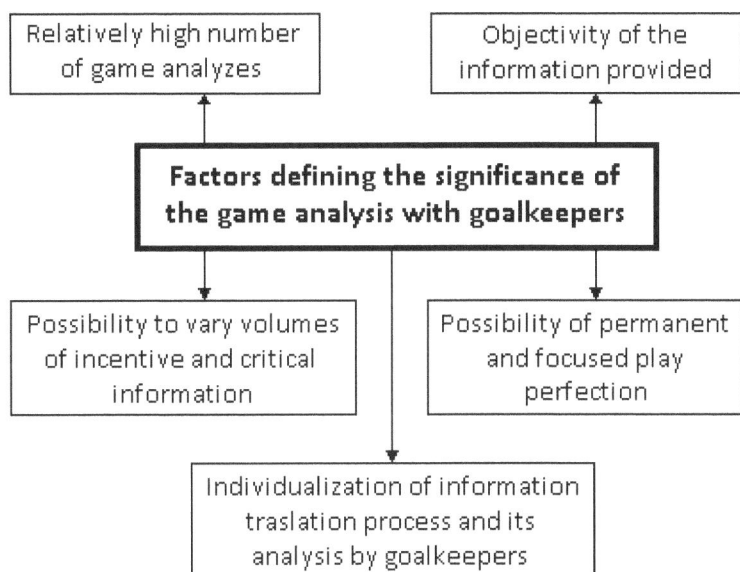

Fig. 24. Main factors defining the significance of the game analysis with goalkeepers for increasing the level of their prowess

For this purpose each match should be considered in terms of principles of the attacking and defensive play construction, and it is particularly important to find out and classify the goalkeepers' play issues of systemic nature during the game analysis.

Thirdly, the information goalkeepers receive during the game analysis is objective.

Gone are those days when coaches had to analyze the game with players basing only on their visual memory data. Now there is possibility to use, besides game visuals, the statistics on goalkeepers' technical and tactical and motion activity in games, registered and analyzed by experts not only from the certain club, but also out of club organizations.

The difficulty is only to select the optimal number of figures from many of presented and construe them correctly.

Fourthly, the game analysis with goalkeepers may be personalized, allowing to improve quality of data for theoretical training. This is due to the fact that the detailed consideration of various nuances of individual and group actions of players at team meeting often has no practical interest for goalkeepers.

Fifthly, there is possibility to present information of critical nature to goalkeepers in the right amount without hurting their authority in the team in the context of the individual game analysis.

It happened that during the team game analysis mainly considered are various in-field players' mistakes. This is done in order to exclude or at least minimize incorrect actions in the future.

Sometimes pointing out at players' mistakes and faults in play may present the criticism of players in a varying degree not only in terms of their playing activity, but personal qualities and abilities (intelligence, courage, volitional powers, talent).

Critical analysis of goalkeepers' play is also a necessary condition for their progress. Taking into account goalkeepers' special status and mentality, though, it is better to analyze their serious mistakes individually to avoid hurting their authority in the team, in these cases volumes of the information of critical and incentive nature may be varied depending on current developments.

5. 2. Defining the time
of analyzing the game
in inter-playing round

The game analysis is not important as such, but as a step on a way of improving the goalkeepers' play quality and achieving victory in the next match. Therefore it is important to define the time of its performing in inter-playing round properly.

It is inappropriate to analyze the game too early or too late relative to its end. This is explained by the following.

In case the game analysis is planned for the very next day after the game, then:

– it hard enough to assess their and their partners' action precisely for goalkeepers who didn't recover after the game for such a short time yet, especially after unsuccessful matches;

– coaches who need to link together various impressions on the game, analyze statistics, determine issues in team play and ways of its solving, may just no get in time physically to get prepared to the theoretical training in full because of time shortage.

In case the game is analyzed with goalkeepers four or five days after, then:

– to this moment they lose interest to this game that goes down in history regardless of the result, and all thoughts are focused on the oncoming one;

– missed are several trainings in which goalkeepers could have performed understanding the feasibility and necessity of performance of suggested drills with due consideration of the last game.

Therefore whilst sufficiently lengthy inter-playing round (seven days and more) we may consider the third day after the game before the beginning of the general training of this cycle as the most appropriate time for game analysis with both goalkeepers and in-field players.

In this case there are more opportunities to solute the identified issues in the preparedness and play actions of players and the team as a whole and to prepare to the oncoming game better.

5. 3. The position of the layout of the football pitch during the game analysis

For many decades in professional teams it is customary to mount the layouts of the football pitch generally horizontal along the length of the pitch.

Most probably it is done by analogy with how they dispose chalkboards in institutions, or probably because it is easier to mount the layout that way technically.

While disposing the layout horizontal along the length of the pitch the visual perception of specified game events corresponds with coaches' vision during the game. This is explained by the following.

In football directions of players' and the ball movements are various, though the general vector of game playing, conditioned upon the shape of the football pitch and the goal position, is from one goal-line to another in parallel with the long axis of the pitch.

In the context of this vector coaches usually positioned at the sideline not far from the point of its intersection with the halfway line visually perceive play moments as to the left or to the right of them, while players, let alone goalkeepers, as closer or further from them (fig. 25).

Inevitably, mounting of the layout horizontal along the length of the pitch is more useful for the coaches than for the players.

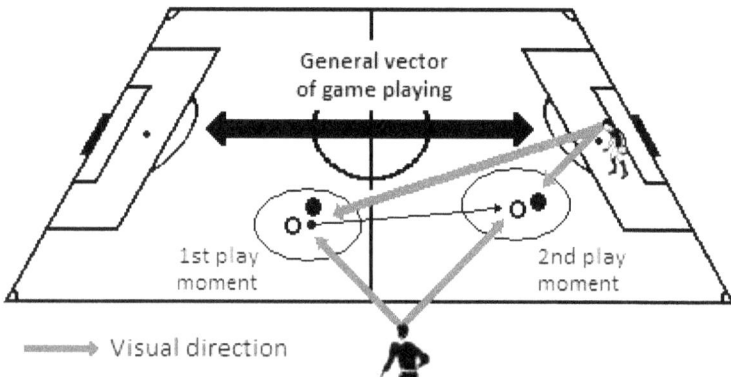

Fig. 25. Visual perception of play moments by coaches and goalkeepers in the context of the general vector of game playing

In this case goalkeepers have to rotate this «game image», shown to them at such layout, imaginatively 90 degrees to project it on the pitch.

Indicative in this context are situations when while analyzing the game the coach suggests that the goalkeeper should «come up to the 18-yard box line» to cover his partners, but at the same time removes the item representing the goalkeeper or draws the needed player's movement in a horizontal plane.

It is reasonably to dispose the layouts of the football pitch vertical along the length of the pitch to create the most comfortable conditions for goalkeepers while analyzing the game for information reception and analysis, and particularly for the compliance in the visual perception of game events on the pitch and demonstrated on the layout (fig. 26).

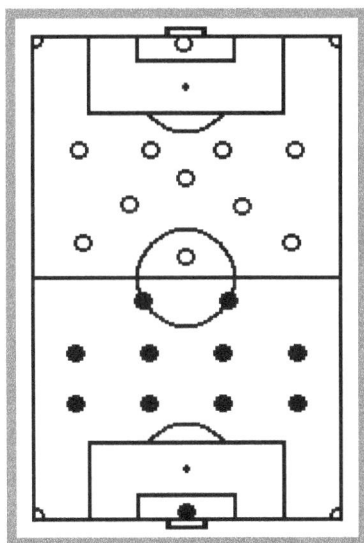

Fig. 26. The position of the layout of the football pitch (vertical along the length of the pitch) in which there is a compliance in goalkeepers' visual perception of game events on the pitch and demonstrated on the layout

5. 4. Coaches' analytical preparation to the game analysis

In order with the game analysis with goalkeepers becomes another starting point on a way of their prowess perfection, they should obtain a well founded information on their play quality, play and preparedness issues and ways of solution.

While preparing such information it is necessary to solve following issues.

First. To define the quality of the goalkeeper's play as a whole and in various periods of the match.

Second. To compile a video set of play situations with the goalkeeper's actions, most important in the context of the result and observance of the principles of play construction by the team.

Third. To specify the problems in the goalkeeper's play and preparedness (define system errors in play actions, gaps in preparedness).

Fourth. To enunciate the main strands of training work on solution of defined play problems and gaps in the goalkeeper's preparedness (in the context of the short term and taking into account the fact of the team performing the another competitive match).

Fifth. To prepare to the developments when probably it will be necessary to lift the goalkeeper's spirit, strengthen his self confidence in correctness of chosen team play conception, encourage players to hard yet necessary training work (the probability of this is the highest during unsuccessful matches).

While preparing to the game analysis with goalkeepers, it is important to analyze all the available information on the game: With that the priority has to be placed on objective data, which may both confirm and disprove subjective impression of their actions.

5. 5. Organizational forms of the game analysis

The practice of professional football teams functioning shows there are several organizational forms of the game analysis with goalkeepers.

Firstly, it is necessary for goalkeepers to participate in the team game analysis, secondly, they may be involved in the game analysis with the defensive players group, thirdly, the game analysis with several team goalkeepers is possible, and fourthly, the individual game analysis with the goalkeeper played the game (fig. 27).

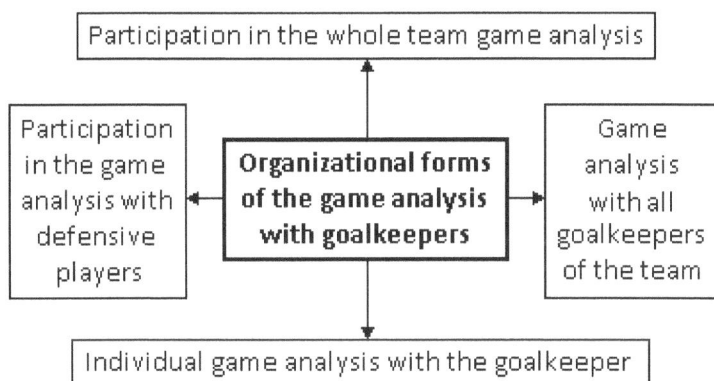

Fig. 27. Possible organizational forms of the game analysis with goalkeepers

As for the first two organizational forms of the game analysis, in these cases the goalkeeper's actions are generally not addressed at all, or considered only in the context of his participation in defensive and attacking collective actions.

Concerning the game analysis with several goalkeepers we may note the following.

During the goalkeepers' play analysis it is almost customary to consider their various play mistakes. With that the specificity of the goalkeeper's position stipulates specific (causes by the competing) and sometimes relatively complicated relationship of goalkeepers in team. In this regard it seems not quite ethical to analyze the game played by the one of goalkeepers among other goalkeepers.

Therefore, from four possible organizational forms of the goalkeeper's play analysis the one when the analysis is executed with the goalkeeper individually is the most appropriate.

5. 6. Game analyzing algorithm

The success of perception of information by goalkeepers during the game analysis is related to logical sequence of its presentation as well.

Such sequence may be observed, if we stick to universal algorithm of theoretical training, which suggests allocation of the opening, main and concluding parts.

The main part of the game analysis may include three information units in its turn:

a) overall assessment of various components of the goalkeeper's play – «the beginning point»;

b) the analysis of correct and wrong goalkeeper's actions («positives and issues»);

c) ways of solving problems in the goalkeeper's play and preparedness – «suggestions»(fig. 28).

Tasks and content of the opening part of analyzing the game

In the opening part of the game analysis with the goalkeeper it is necessary to set him on a working mood, briefly explain main problems and report about the approximate time of this theoretical training.

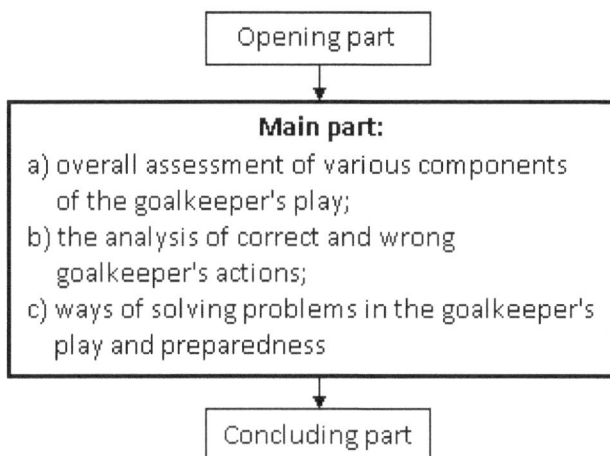

Fig. 28. Algorithm of the game analysis with goalkeepers

It is important to keep within the announced schedule of the lesson later on, as in this case there will be greater attention of the goalkeeper trusting the coach at following game analysis.

In case the goalkeeper's attention is distracted with something at the beginning of the game analysis. it is important to help him to put irrelevant thoughts and worries aside and focus exactly on the game analysis.

There is an opinion it is necessary to find a spot for a joke or a quirk to create a favorable working environment at this moment. Basically it is a fine way to begin the game analysis, though it is better to apply it ad hoc and not constantly.

Tasks and content of main part of analyzing the game

The tasks of the main part of the game analysis with the goalkeeper consist in analysis of his play and informing him about the directions of training work in the short term. These tasks may be completed with the sequential consideration of three following information units.

First information unit – «the beginning point». Overall assessment of the goalkeeper's play actions quality may become «the beginning point» for the analysis of his play.

It is reasonable to characterize as a whole his:
– actions in defense and attack;
– play characteristics in various periods of the game;
– psychoemotional characteristics of behavior in the game.

It is best if overall assessment of the goalkeeper's play is based not only on subjective judgments, but also on some statistical information.

Second information unit – «positives and issues». Any goalkeeper has a certain number of correct and wrong to different extent actions in every game. Either actions should be analyzed, so the goalkeeper could improve his prowess.

Taking this into account, it is necessary to make emphasis on the considering of correct and wrong goalkeeper's actions in attack and defense and formalization of main issues in his play and preparedness in the second information unit of the main part of game analysis.

During the analysis of the goalkeeper's defensive play the attention is turned to the «positives and issues» in his actions during the opponent's attacks, performed in open play and from set pieces, in which:
– goals were scored or goalscoring chances created (considered are all goalkeeper's actions, ideally from the beginning of such attacks and necessarily coupled with partners' actions);
– there were shots on goal, passes towards the goal and attempts to outplay the goalkeeper (assessed are the goalkeeper's positioning along the length and across the width of the pitch, good timing of movements, technique of catching and blocking the ball, managing the team defensive actions);
– there were no shots on goal, passes towards the goal and attempts to outplay the goalkeeper (analyzed are the goalkeeper's positioning along the length and across the width of the pitch and managing the team defensive actions).

The goalkeeper's attacking play should be considered from following positions:

– managing partners' actions;

– performing the role of a mainstay for keeping the possession over the ball;

– quality of passes with a foot in open play;

– putting the ball into play with a goal-kick according to the game plan;

– good timing, precision and reasonability of passes with a hand;

– control over the course of the game.

In conclusion of the second information unit in the main part of the game analysis we should briefly enunciate the main issues in team's play and preparedness (typical mistakes of fundamental nature in play actions, weaknesses in preparedness).

Third information unit – «suggestions». This information unit presents a familiarization of the goalkeeper with issues needed to be solved during the preparation to the following match and the main strands of training work during that period.

Tasks and content of the concluding part of the game analysis

In the concluding part of the game analysis we should summarize all the considered stuff and motivate the goalkeeper towards the next training work, assure him it would necessary deliver. It is reasonable to finish the game analysis on a positive note regardless of how the game ends.

5. 7. Methodological recommendations on analyzing the game

During the game analysis with goalkeepers it is important to stick to several following rules.

1. To use such terminology and intonation that goalkeepers understand what is said in a way the coach wants.

2. It is better to express criticism in a quiet, friendly tone. Criticism should obligingly be fair and confirmed with objective data providing a positive background for discussion of mistakes and way of solving.

3. Not to waste attention on minor moments and issues far from the main strand of the game analysis.

4. To lead goalkeepers to positive conclusions on course of the game analysis, joining own opinion with their, unless they discord crucially.

5. To prompt goalkeepers to analyze the status quo and how they would realize the attitudes, received at the game analysis, later by themselves.

For notes

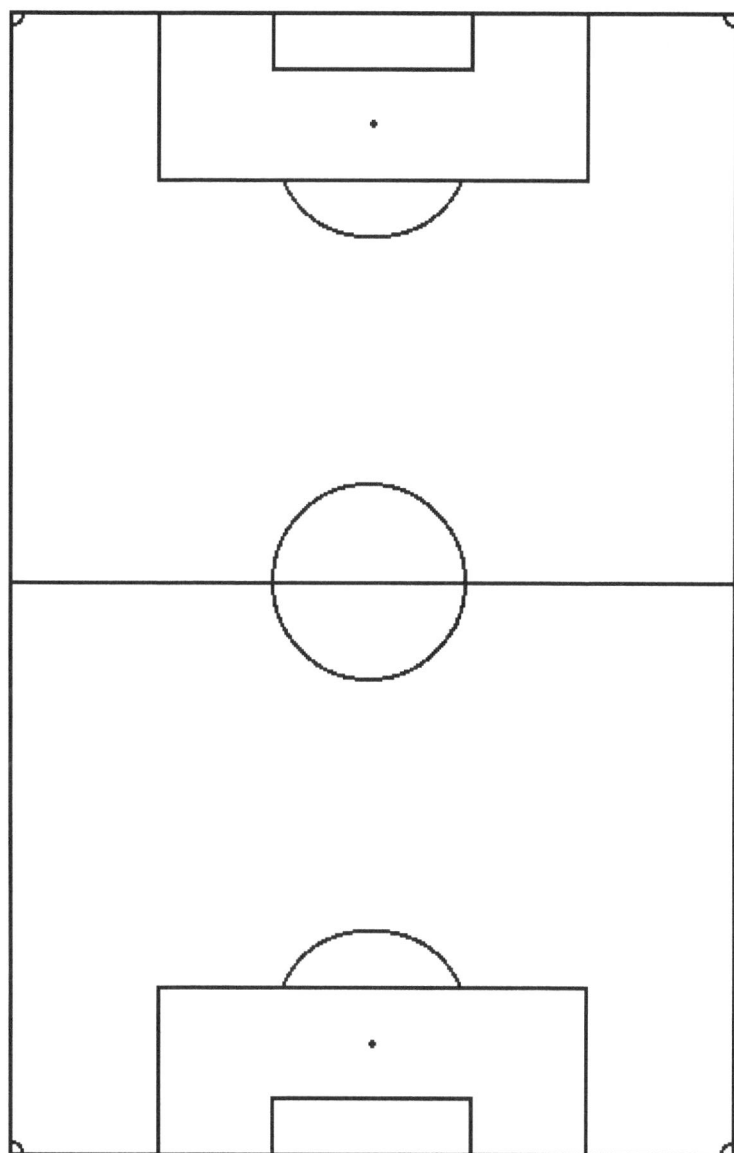

CHAPTER 6.
ACQUIRING OF KNOWLEDGE
ON VARIOUS ISSUES OF
THEIR PREPARATION AND
HEALTH PRESERVATION
BY GOALKEEPERS

Gaining knowledge about various aspects of their training and health preservation is an important component of the goalkeepers' theoretical training. Relevance of this knowledge for goalkeepers is due to several reasons.

First. The efficiency of the goalkeepers' preparation and play as a result increase with their active and creative involvement in the training process. Conscious activity and creativity are possible if goalkeepers know, which qualities and abilities are developed and improved while performing one or another drill.

Second. The familiarization of goalkeepers with information revealing pedagogical and medical aspects of their health preservation is necessary since cases of getting injured occur more often on training than in competitive games, and even experienced players should be protected from performing high-injury actions (random or during drills).

Third. Some goalkeepers, pondering on coaching work, begin to try to understand its specificity. Information on general principles and methods of sport training and its particular laws appearing in football would help them to theoretically comprehend the content and organization of the training process, understand the logic of coaching work. Naturally, it is important to pay particular attention to these goalkeepers in the context of volume and depth of delivery of relevant information.

For understanding of main issues of their training and health preservation it is important for goalkeepers to have an idea:

– on basic components of the goalkeeper's play prowess (specific anticipation reactions, technique and tactics, motor characteristics and functional capabilities) and methods of its perfection;

– on basics of development of the training (certain training spell, cycles between games and training cycles of various duration, stages of year cycle of training);

– on anatomic, physiological and biochemical machinery of sport motion activity;

– on methods and sources of psychological training (managing the psychic distress, motivation stimulation, development of psychological stability and ability to keep the absorption);

– on the culture of daily diet and water schedule, using sport nutrition special products;

– on pedagogical and medical preventive means of injuries and disease, sport rehabilitation.

Disclosure of these issues may take place:

– directly on course of training, when one or another exercise tallies with certain theoretical knowledge;

– in the context of such forms of theoretical trainings as a conversation, message and discussion, analysis of trainings and certain drills;

– with the goalkeepers' self-study of professional literature and footage on the theory and method of football and sport training.

It is preferable for goalkeepers to receive the information on these issues quite systematically and with certain methodological sentence.

AFTERWORD

First. As a whole, training of players may be considered from different perspectives, and among other things we may mark also the theoretical part besides the practical.

Theoretical training of goalkeepers includes several main directions of work. Some of these direction are directly linked with competitive games, as they suggest the analytical preparation to the game, game guideline and analysis of played game.

Theoretical training in other directions may help towards the perfection of the goalkeepers' prowess indirectly through further understanding of football, principles and methods of training, issues of health preservation.

Second. In any game goalkeepers may have definite complications while performing their responsibilities, from whence the probability of them making wrong decisions increases.

Possibilities of overcoming those difficulties goalkeepers may meet with on course of the game largely depend on the quality of their analytical preparation to the game, suggesting consideration of the specificity of the match, analysis of information on the opponent's play construction and defining the optimal tactics of own actions in the game.

Third. The game guideline for goalkeepers is exercised few hours ahead of the match in order to bring them to the game fully prepared in the theoretical and psychological context. Goalkeepers may receive necessary information on the opponent's team and certain players, own team play construction, own behavior and actions in various play situation individually, and also participating in the game guideline for the whole team or just for the defense.

Fourth. Game analysis with goalkeepers is potentially effective recipe of increasing the level of their prowess.

This is due to the fact they may be provided with information of their play quality, play issues and preparedness and ways of solution of these problems.

While preparing to the game analysis with goalkeepers the priority has to be placed on objective data, which may both confirm and disprove subjective impressions of their play activity.

The task of the game analysis is not only to analyze of previous match and present a project for further work, but also to create atmosphere of interest for goalkeepers in permanent improvement of sport mastery as a necessary condition of their progress.

Fifth. For well-timed and proper organization of the goal defense it is important for goalkeepers to be able to anticipate the opponents actions. Knowing the statistical regularities of football reflecting greater or smaller probability of various events and consequently greater or smaller efficiency of one or another variant of players' actions in competitive games may help them in this context.

Taking into account three kinds of specific goalkeeper anticipation reactions, these regularities may be classified into three groups, specifically as attributes of:

– probable course of the game and development of certain play situations;

– probable moment, speed and direction of sending the ball by players towards the goal and while shooting on goal;

– probable trajectory of the ball flying while shooting on goal.

Knowing the regularities of football may also help goalkeepers to correct the work on improving of anticipation reactions and certain components of tactical and technical preparedness in the context of self training.

Sixth. Knowing various issues of their training and health preservation allows goalkeepers to theoretically comprehend the content and organization of the training process, increase the efficiency of training and play prowess consequently, minimize the probability of injuries and disease.

It is important to pay particular attention to goalkeepers who show interest in coaching work and begin to try to understand its specificity in the context of volume and depth of delivery of relevant information.

BIBLIOGRAPHY

Акимов А. Игра футбольного вратаря / А. Акимов. – М.: Физкультура и спорт, 1978. – 95 с.

Арестов Ю.М. и др. Особенности соревновательной деятельности и методика тренировки юных вратарей в футболе: метод. рекомендации / Ю.М. Арестов, М.А. Годик, А.И. Шамардин, А.М. Четырко. – М., ГЦОЛИФК, 1979. – 28 с.

Аркадьев Б.А. Тактика футбольной игры / Б.А. Аркадьев. – М.: Физкультура и спорт, 1962. – 168 с.

Воронова В. Психологическое сопровождение спортивной деятельности в футболе / В. Воронова. – Киев, Научно-метод. (технический) комитет Федерации футбола Украины. – 2001. – 137 с.

Голомазов С., Чирва Б. Футбол. Тренировка вратаря / С. Голомазов, Б. Чирва. – М., РГАФК, 1996. – 200 с.

Голомазов С.В., Чирва Б.Г. Футбол. Антиципация в игре вратарей / С.В. Голомазов, Б.Г. Чирва. – М.: ТВТ Дивизион, 2008. – 80 с.

Горский Л. Игра хоккейного вратаря / Л. Горский. – М.: Физкультура и спорт, 1974. – 142 с.

Иванин А.Г., Преображенский И.Н. Методы теоретической подготовки / А.Г. Иванин, И.Н. Преображенский // Пути совершенствования спортивного мастерства. – М.: Физкультура и спорт, 1966. – С. 76-95.

Качалин Г.Д. Тактика футбола / Г.Д. Качалин. – М.: Физкультура и спорт, 1986. – 128 с.

Ковтученко А.И. Некоторые статистические закономерности в футболе / А.И. Ковтученко // Теория и практика физической культуры. – 1975. – № 1. – С. 20-22.

Кочетков А.П. Управление футбольной командой / А.П. Кочетков. – М.: ООО «Астрель»: ООО «Издательство АСТ», 2002. – 192 с.

Красножан Ю.А., Чирва Б.Г. Футбол. Разбор игры с футболистами профессиональной команды / Ю.А. Красножан, Б.Г. Чирва. – М.: ТВТ Дивизион, 2013. – 68 с.

Рымашевский Г.А. Управление командой в соревнованиях по футболу / Г.А. Рымашевский // Проблемы спорта высших достижений и подготовки спортивного резерва: материалы научно-практ. конференции. – Минск, 1993. – С. 70-74.

Соломонко В.В. Тренировка вратаря в футболе / В.В. Соломонко. – Киев: Здоров'я, 1986. – 124 с.

Спортивная метрология: учебник для ин-тов физ. культуры / Под ред. В.М. Зациорского. – М.: Физкультура и спорт, 1982. – 250 с.

Стернин И.А. Практическая риторика / И.А. Стернин. – М.: Издательский центр «Академия», 2008. – 272 с.

Тунис М. Психология вратаря / М. Тунис. – М.: «Человек», 2010. – 128 с.

Управление командой в процессе соревнований / В книге: Баскетбол: учебник для ин-тов физ. культуры. – М.: Физкультура и спорт, 1976. – С. 229-234.

Фролова М.И. Психолого-педагогические основы руководства спортивной командой: метод. разработка по спецкурсу для студентов ИФК / М.И. Фролова. – М.: РИО ГЦОЛИФК, 1980. – 16 с.

Футбол: учебник для ин-тов физ. культуры / Под ред. М.С. Полишкиса и В.А. Выжгина. – М.: Физкультура, образование и наука, 1999. – 253 с.

Ханин Ю.Л. Психология общения в спорте / Ю.Л. Ханин. – М.: Физкультура и спорт, 1980. – 206 с.

Чирва Б.Г. Аналитические закономерности игры в футбол как основа для выбора тактики игры и построения технико-тактической подготовки квалифицированных футболистов / Б.Г. Чирва // Теория и практика физической культуры. – 2006. – № 7. – С. 28-29.

Чирва Б.Г. Футбол. Концепция технической и тактической подготовки футболистов / Б.Г. Чирва. – М.: ТВТ Дивизион, 2008. – 336 с.

Чирва Б.Г., Красножан Ю.А. Футбол. Подготовка и проведение разбора игр с футболистами: метод. разработки для тренеров. Выпуск 39 / Б.Г. Чирва, Ю.А. Красножан. – М., РГУФКСМиТ, 2012. – 44 с.

ENCLOSURE

Volume of victories (per cent of number of games in which goals were scored) of teams scored first in various time periods in various competitions during 2006-2013 (following the normal time of 1266 games)

Competitions	Volume of victories (per cent) of teams scored first in intervals of the game	
	from 1st to 25th minute	from 26th to 90th minute
World Cup 2006	41	30
Euro-2008	36	39
Russian Premier-League 2009	33	42
World Cup 2010	34	43
Russian Premier-League 2010	31	37
Russian Premier-League 2011-12	30	40
Euro-2012	45	35
Russian Premier-League 2012-13	35	36

Volume of goalscoring attacks (as a percentage of total) beginning after a tackle or interception of the ball in various areas of the pitch, and their duration (sec) at the World Cup 1998

Figures	Point of the attacks beginning		
	defensive zone	middle zone	attacking zone
Volume of attacks (%)	42	33	25
Duration of attacks (sec) (average data and variability	20 (8-40)	13 (7-50)	7 (3-14)

Volume of victories, draws and defeats (per cent of number of games in which goals were scored) of teams scored first in various time periods in various competitions during World Cup 2010 (following the normal time of games)

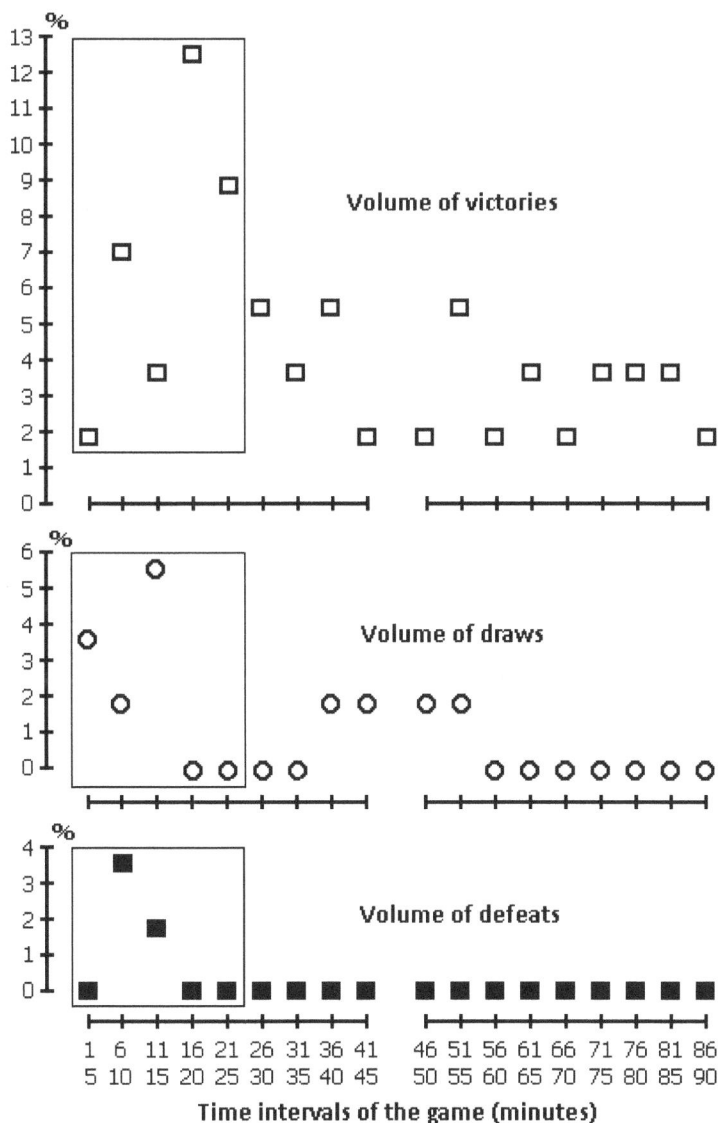

Time intervals of the game (minutes)

Frequency of cases (as a percentage of total cases) when teams scored their second goal at various intervals of time in matches of Russian Championship, in case these goals were first and second in the game for these teams (following 270 cases)

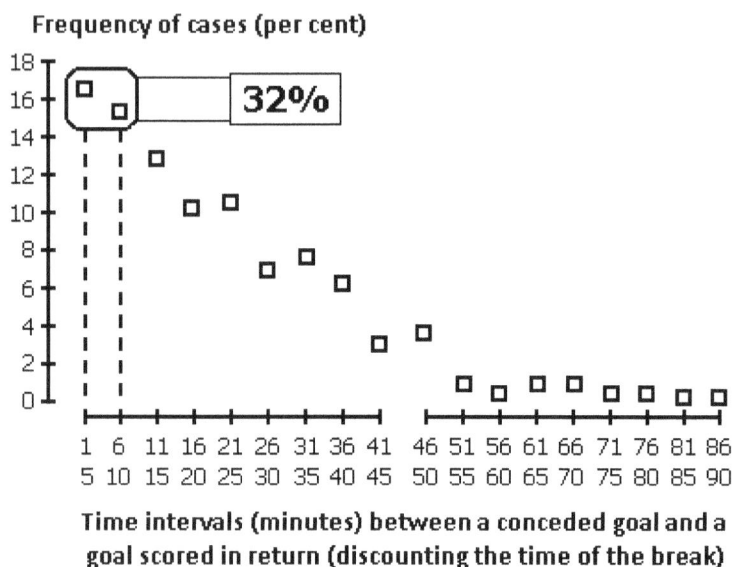

Frequency of cases (per cent)

32%

Time intervals (minutes) between a conceded goal and a goal scored in return (discounting the time of the break)

Points relevant to areas on the pitch from which headers were scored at the World Cup 1998

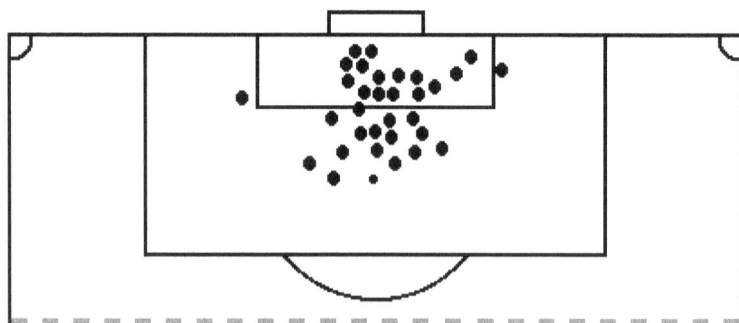

Frequency of cases (as a percentage of total cases) when teams scored a goal in return after conceded goal at various intervals of time in matches of Russian Championship (following 160 cases)

Frequency of cases (per cent)

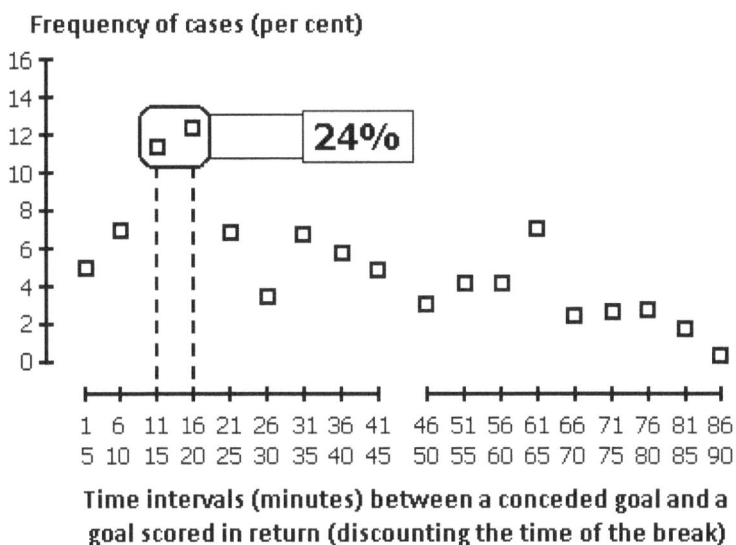

Time intervals (minutes) between a conceded goal and a goal scored in return (discounting the time of the break)

Points relevant to areas on the pitch from which goals were scored with a foot in open play in the 18-yard box at the World Cup 1998

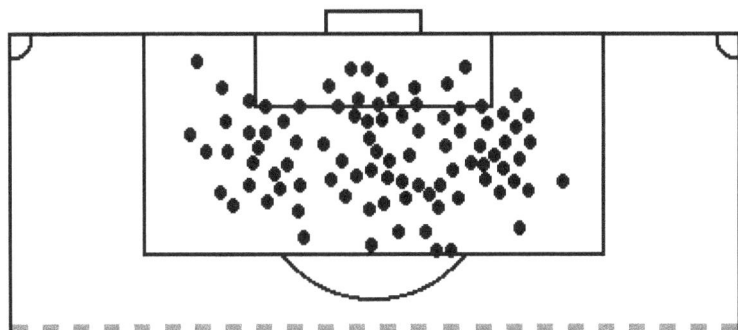

75

Points relevant to areas on the pitch from which 90% of assists, direction of passes and point of reception of the ball at the World Cup 1998

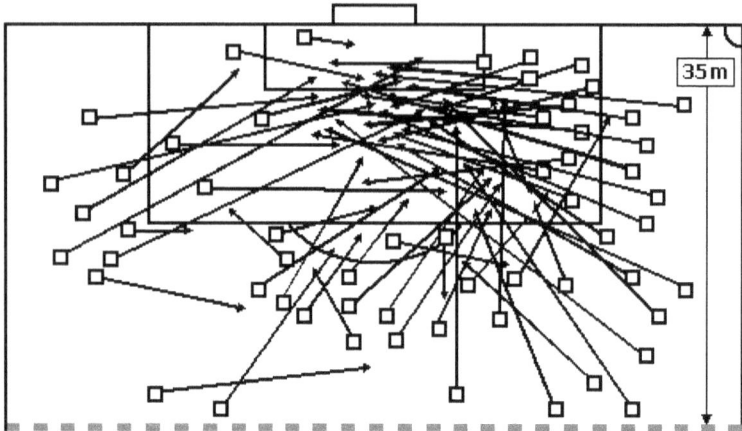

Volume of goals (as a percentage of total) scored from the goal area, 18-yard box and outside of the box in games of World Cup and European Championship during 1990-2012

Competitions	Volume of goals (%) scored		
	from the goal area	from the 18-yard box (excluding the goal area)	from the outside of the 18-yard box
World Cup 1990	24	64	12
World Cup 1994	14	67	19
Euro-1996	11	77	12
World Cup 1998	18	69	13
Euro-2000	20	63	17
World Cup 2002	24	59	17
Euro-2004	23	64	13
World Cup 2006	22	60	18
Euro-2008	25	69	6
World Cup 2010	21	62	17
Euro-2012	20	68	12

Points relevant to areas on the pitch from which goals were scored with a foot at Euro-2008 (excluding goals scored from the spot)

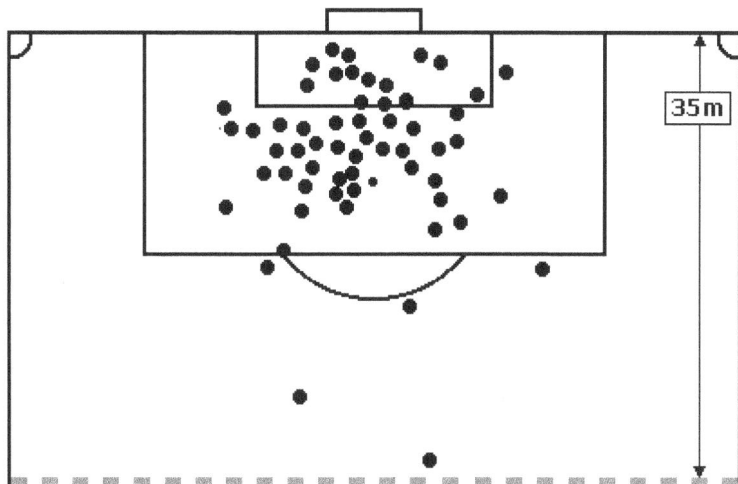

Points relevant to areas on the pitch from which headers were scored at the World Cup 2008

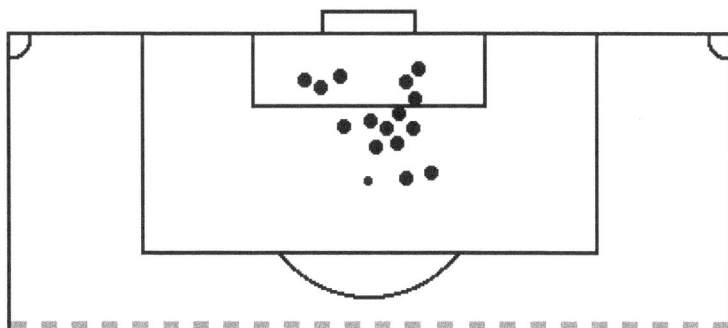

www.ingramcontent.com/pod-product-compliance
Lightning Source LLC
Chambersburg PA
CBHW071929020426
42331CB00010B/2785